Shakespeare for Contemporary Theatre

Volume 3

Twelfth Night

&

Favorite Monologues

by William Shakespeare

adapted by Jane Farnol

© 2023 Jane Farnol

Shakespeare for Contemporary Theatre
Volume 3

Twelfth Night
&
Favorite Monologues

by William Shakespeare

adapted by Jane Farnol

Published by

ARKETT PUBLISHING
division of Arkettype
PO Box 36, Gaylordsville, CT 06755
806-350-4007 • Fax 860-355-3970
www.local-author.com

Copyright © 2023 Jane Farnol

All rights reserved under International and Pan-American Copyright Conventions. No part of this book may be reproduced or transmitted by any means without permission in writing from the author. See inside for performance rights, billing, and credit requirements.

ISBN 979-8-8690-6427-1

Printed in USA.

Cover photos: Front—Sean Latasa as Malvolio with Tim Breslin as Sir Andrew in the background. Back—Jennifer Wallace as Viola with Jimmy Collins as Sea Captain in "Twelfth Night" at Brookfield Theatre © 2023 Stephen Cihanek - www.Cihanek.com

Foreword

The plays of William Shakespeare remain the most popular to perform on any stage. The reasons for this are many including the timelessness of the plays' themes and exceptional writing. Theatres also appreciate that the plays allow for unlimited creativity while also being affordable to perform. The problems with staging his plays include the extensive casts and the long performance times. In Shakespeare's time, a play of three or more hours was common. Current audiences prefer plays that are one to two hours long.

In "Shakespeare for Contemporary Theatre" Jane Farnol takes some of Shakespeare's most loved plays and edits them down to suit modern needs. This volume includes "Twelfth Night" and a series of monologues designed to be performed in sequence for an evening of Shakespeare. Both are designed to keep cast lists flexible and scripts are edited to focus on action while maintaining the bard's style and language. The result is a performance that moves well and is accessible for modern theatre companies to perform.

Additionally, there is no licensing fee to perform these edited versions as long as a credit is included in show programs. Directors are free to innovate as their situation allows. The monologues are perfect for study or audition purposes with a wide range of tone and character to choose from.

Important Billing & Credit Requirements

Theatre groups are welcome to perform any of the scripts in this volume with the following program credits:

Show Title
by William Shakespeare
adapted by Jane Farnol

About Jane Farnol

Jane Farnol was born in England and trained at the Royal Academy of Dramatic Art and Elmhurst Ballet School. She is the great-niece of Jeffery Farnol, the author of many romance novels including *The Broad Highway* and *The Money Moon*. At RADA, she developed an abiding love of Shakespeare under the tutelage of octogenarian Miss Nell Carter. Her New York acting credits include Teresa in Brendan Behan's *The Hostage* at the Sheridan Square Playhouse, the Chorus in *The Trojan Women* directed by Theodore Mann at Circle in the Square, and Ann in the Broadway production of *Hail Scrawdyke!* directed by Alan Arkin. At the American Shakespeare Festival Theatre in Stratford, Connecticut, her roles ranged from Titania in *A Midsummer Night's Dream* playing opposite to and directed by Cyril Ritchard, to Lady Macbeth in *Macbeth* directed by John Houseman. On television, Jane had running roles on *The Guiding Light* and *As The World Turns*. Jane's movie *The Colonial Naturalist* is shown as a permanent feature at Colonial Williamsburg. At WCBS Radio, Jane was Dave Garroway's assistant and Executive Director of Lee Theodore's *American Dance Machine*. Since moving to Connecticut Jane has directed over thirty-five plays in eighteen years at various venues.

Twelfth Night at Brookfield Theatre

By William Shakespeare, adapted and directed by Jane Farnol, set design Andrew Okell, costumes Lou Okell. All photos by **Stephen Cihanek**. *Contact Stephen@Cihanek.com for more information or visit www.Cihanek.com.*

"Conceal me what I am."

"Tell me if this be the lady of the house..."

"He will fight with you for 's oath sake."

"...and so look to thyself."

"I am a dog at a catch."

"Be not afraid of greatness."

"What employment have we here?" "He is in yellow stockings!"

"A sister, you are she!"

"Here is my hand."

Table of Contents

Twelfth Night
Characters & Scenes 9
Twelfth Night 10-94
Feste's Song: *The Wind & The Rain* 95

Favorite Monologues
Notes On Performing 96
Table of Contents 97
The Monologues 98–143

Twelfth Night
by William Shakespeare
adapted by Jane Farnol

ACT I 10

ACT II 52

SETTING
The coast, countryside, and town of Illyria

PRODUCTION NOTES

This adaptation was developed for Brookfield Theatre and was produced in September 2023. The script has been edited to focus on the action, combine scenes, and limit cast size.

CAST

Viola	Jennifer Wallace
Sea Captain	Jimmy Collins
Sebastian	Sergio Arguelles
Antonio	Chris Fay
Orsino	Sean Gorman
Olivia	Céline Montaudy
Maria	Stacy-Lee Frome
Sir Toby Belch	Thomas Samuels
Sir Andrew Aguecheek	Tim Breslin
Malvolio	Sean Latasa
Feste	Tyler Small
Fabian	Jack Hoyt
Valentine	Jackson Turner
Priest	Tom Heydenburg
Officer	Ron Malyszka

Twelfth Night
by William Shakespeare
adapted by Jane Farnol

CHARACTERS

VIOLA, a lady of Messaline (later disguised as CESARIO)
SEA CAPTAIN, friend to Viola
SEBASTIAN, Viola's brother
ANTONIO, sea captain and friend to Sebastian
ORSINO, Duke of Illyria
OLIVIA, an Illyrian countess
MARIA, her gentlewoman
SIR TOBY BELCH, Olivia's kinsman
SIR ANDREW AGUECHEEK, Sir Toby's companion
MALVOLIO, steward in Olivia's household
FESTE, Olivia's jester
FABIAN, a gentleman in Olivia's household
VALENTINE, a gentleman serving Orsino
PRIEST
OFFICER
Lords, Sailors, Musicians, and other Attendants as needed

SCENES

A city in Illyria near the sea coast. Set should be simple and scenes should flow from one to the next without set change.

ACT 1

[Enter VIOLA and CAPTAIN]

VIOLA
What country, friend, is this?

CAPTAIN
This is Illyria, lady.

VIOLA
And what should I do in Illyria?
My brother he is in Elysium.
Perchance he is not drowned—What think you, Captain?

CAPTAIN
It is perchance that you yourself were saved.

VIOLA
O, my poor brother! And so perchance may he be.

CAPTAIN
True, madam. And to comfort you with chance,
Assure yourself, after our ship did split,
When you and those poor number saved with you
Hung on our driving boat, I saw your brother,
Most provident in peril, bind himself
To a strong mast that lived upon the sea,
Where, like Arion on the dolphin's back,
I saw him hold acquaintance with the waves
So long as I could see.

VIOLA *[giving him money]* For saying so, there's gold.
Know'st thou this country?

CAPTAIN
Ay, madam, well, for I was bred and born
Not three hours' travel from this very place.

VIOLA
Who governs here?

CAPTAIN
A noble duke, in nature as in name.

VIOLA
What is his name?

CAPTAIN
Orsino.

VIOLA
Orsino. I have heard my father name him.
He was a bachelor then.

CAPTAIN
And so is now, or was so very late;
For but a month ago I went from hence,
And then 'twas fresh in murmur (as, you know,
What great ones do the less will prattle of)
That he did seek the love of fair Olivia.

VIOLA
What's she?

CAPTAIN
A virtuous maid, the daughter of a count
That died some twelvemonth since, then leaving her
In the protection of his son, her brother,
Who shortly also died, for whose dear love,
They say, she hath abjured the sight
And company of men.

VIOLA
O, that I served that lady,
And might not be delivered to the world
Till I had made mine own occasion mellow,
What my estate is.

CAPTAIN
That were hard to compass
Because she will admit no kind of suit,
No, not the Duke's.

VIOLA
There is a fair behavior in thee, captain,
I prithee—and I'll pay thee bounteously—
Conceal me what I am, and be my aid
For such disguise as haply shall become
The form of my intent. I'll serve this duke.
Thou shalt present me as an eunuch to him.
It may be worth thy pains, for I can sing
And speak to him in many sorts of music
That will allow me very worth his service.

What else may hap, to time I will commit.
Only shape thou thy silence to my wit.

CAPTAIN
Be you his eunuch, and your mute I'll be.
When my tongue blabs, then let mine eyes not see.

VIOLA
I thank thee. Lead me on.

[EXIT]

[Enter ORSINO, Duke of Illyria, and FESTE playing music]

ORSINO
If music be the food of love, play on.
Give me excess of it, that, surfeiting,
The appetite may sicken and so die.
That strain again! It had a dying fall.
O, it came o'er my ear like the sweet sound
That breathes upon a bank of violets,
Stealing and giving odor. Enough; no more.
(music ends)
'Tis not so sweet now as it was before.
O spirit of love, how quick and fresh art thou,
That, notwithstanding thy capacity
Receiveth as the sea, naught enters there,
Of what validity and pitch soe'er,
But falls into abatement and low price
Even in a minute. So full of shapes is fancy
That it alone is high fantastical.

FESTE
Will you go hunt, my lord?

ORSINO
What, Fool?

FESTE
The hart.

ORSINO
Why, so I do, the noblest that I have.
O, when mine eyes did see Olivia first,
Methought she purged the air of pestilence.

That instant was I turned into a hart,
And my desires, like fell and cruel hounds,
E'er since pursue me.

[Enter VALENTINE]

How now, what news from her?

VALENTINE
So please my lord, I might not be admitted,
But from her handmaid do return this answer:
The element itself, till seven years' heat,
Shall not behold her face at ample view,
But like a cloistress she will veiled walk,
And water once a day her chamber round
With eye-offending brine—all this to season
A brother's dead love, which she would keep fresh
And lasting in her sad remembrance.

ORSINO
O, she that hath a heart of that fine frame
To pay this debt of love but to a brother,
How will she love when the rich golden shaft
Hath killed the flock of all affections else
That live in her; when liver, brain, and heart,
These sovereign thrones, are all supplied, and filled
Her sweet perfections with one self king!
Away before me to sweet beds of flowers!
Love thoughts lie rich when canopied with bowers.

[EXIT]

[Enter SIR TOBY and MARIA]

TOBY
What a plague means my niece to take the death
of her brother thus? I am sure care's an enemy to life.

MARIA
By my troth, Sir Toby, you must come in earlier o' nights.
Your cousin, my lady, takes great exceptions to your ill hours.

TOBY
Why, let her except before excepted!

MARIA
Ay, but you must confine yourself within the modest limits of order.

TOBY
Confine? I'll confine myself no finer than I am. These clothes are good enough to drink in, and so be these boots too. An they be not, let them hang themselves in their own straps!

MARIA
That quaffing and drinking will undo you. I heard my lady talk of it yesterday, and of a foolish knight that you brought in one night here to be her wooer.

TOBY
Who, Sir Andrew Aguecheek?

MARIA
Ay, he.

TOBY
He's as tall a man as any 's in Illyria.

MARIA
What's that to th' purpose?

TOBY
Why, he has three thousand ducats a year!

MARIA
Ay, but he'll have but a year in all these ducats.
He's a very fool and a prodigal.

TOBY
Fie that you'll say so! He plays o' th' viol-de-gamboys
and speaks three or four languages word for word
without book, and hath all the good gifts of nature.

MARIA
He hath indeed, almost natural, for, besides that he's a fool, he's a great quarreler, and, but that he hath the gift of a coward to allay the gust he hath in quarreling, 'tis thought among the prudent he would quickly have the gift of a grave.

TOBY
By this hand, they are scoundrels and substractors that say so of him. Who are they?

MARIA
They that add, moreover, he's drunk nightly in your company.

TOBY
With drinking healths to my niece. I'll drink to her as long as there is a passage in my throat and drink in Illyria. What, wench! Castiliano vulgo, for here comes Sir Andrew Agueface.

[Enter Sir Andrew]

ANDREW
Sir Toby Belch! How now, Sir Toby Belch?

TOBY
Sweet Sir Andrew!

ANDREW *[to Maria]*
Bless you, fair shrew.

MARIA
And you too, sir.

TOBY
Accost, Sir Andrew, accost!

ANDREW
What's that?

TOBY
My niece's chambermaid.

ANDREW
Good Mistress Accost, I desire better acquaintance.

MARIA
My name is Mary, sir.

ANDREW
Good Mistress Mary Accost—

TOBY
You mistake, knight. "Accost" is front her, board her, woo her, assail her.

ANDREW
By my troth, I would not undertake her in this company. Is that the meaning of "accost"?

MARIA
Fare you well, gentlemen. *[She begins to exit]*

TOBY
An thou let part so, Sir Andrew, would thou mightst never draw sword again.

ANDREW
An you part so, mistress, I would I might never draw sword again. Fair lady, do you think you have fools in hand?

MARIA
Sir, I have not you by th' hand.

ANDREW
Marry, but you shall have, and here's my hand. *[He offers his hand]*

MARIA *[taking his hand]*
Now sir, thought is free. I pray you, bring your hand to th' butt'ry bar and let it drink.

ANDREW
Wherefore, sweetheart? What's your metaphor?

MARIA
It's dry, sir.

ANDREW
Why, I think so. I am not such an ass but I can keep my hand dry. But what's your jest?

MARIA
A dry jest, sir.

ANDREW
Are you full of them?

MARIA
Ay, sir, I have them at my fingers' ends. Marry, now I let go your hand, I am barren.
                    [MARIA exits]

TOBY
O knight, thou lack'st a cup of canary! When did I see thee so put down?

ANDREW
Never in your life, I think, unless you see canary put me down.
Methinks sometimes I have no more wit than a Christian
or an ordinary man has. But I am a great eater of beef,
and I believe that does harm to my wit.

TOBY
No question.

ANDREW
An I thought that, I'd forswear it. I'll ride home tomorrow, Sir Toby.

TOBY
Pourquoi, my dear knight?

ANDREW
What is "pourquoi"? Do, or not do? I would I had bestowed that time in
the tongues that I have in fencing, dancing, and bearbaiting. O, had I but
followed the arts!

TOBY
Then hadst thou had an excellent head of hair.

ANDREW
Why, would that have mended my hair?

TOBY
Past question, for thou seest it will not curl by nature.

ANDREW
But it becomes me well enough, does 't not?

TOBY
Excellent! It hangs like flax on a distaff, and I hope to see a huswife
take thee between her legs and spin it off.

ANDREW
Faith, I'll home tomorrow, Sir Toby. Your niece will not be seen,
or if she be, it's four to one she'll none of me.
The Count himself here hard by woos her.

TOBY
She'll none o' th' Count. She'll not match above her degree, neither in
estate, years, nor wit. I have heard her swear 't. Tut, there's life in 't, man.

ANDREW
I'll stay a month longer. I am a fellow o' th' strangest mind i' th' world. I delight in masques and revels sometimes altogether.

TOBY
Art thou good at these kickshawses, knight?

ANDREW
As any man in Illyria, whatsoever he be, under the degree of my betters, and yet I will not compare with an old man.

TOBY
What is thy excellence in a galliard, knight?

ANDREW
Faith, I can cut a caper.

TOBY
And I can cut the mutton to 't.

ANDREW
And I think I have the back-trick simply as strong as any man in Illyria.

TOBY
Wherefore are these things hid? Wherefore have these gifts a curtain before 'em? Why dost thou not go to church in a galliard and come home in a coranto? I did think, by the excellent constitution of thy leg, it was formed under the star of a galliard.

ANDREW
Ay, 'tis strong, and it does indifferent well in a dun-colored stock. Shall we set about some revels?

TOBY
What shall we do else? Were we not born under Taurus?

ANDREW
Taurus? That's sides and heart.

TOBY
No, sir, it is legs and thighs. Let me see thee caper. *[Sir Andrew dances]* Ha, higher! Ha, ha, excellent!

[EXIT]

[Enter VALENTINE and VIOLA in man's attire as CESARIO]

VALENTINE
If the Duke continue these favors towards you, Cesario, you are like to be much advanced. He hath known you but three days, and already you are no stranger.

VIOLA
You either fear his humor or my negligence, that you call in question the continuance of his love. Is he inconstant, sir, in his favors?

VALENTINE
No, believe me.

VIOLA
I thank you. Here comes the Count.

[Enter ORSINO]

ORSINO
Who saw Cesario, ho?

VIOLA
On your attendance, my lord, here.

ORSINO *[to Valentine]*
Stand you awhile aloof.—Cesario,
Thou know'st no less but all. I have unclasped
To thee the book even of my secret soul.
Therefore, good youth, address thy gait unto her.
Be not denied access. Stand at her doors
And tell them, there thy fixed foot shall grow
Till thou have audience.

VIOLA
Sure, my noble lord,
If she be so abandoned to her sorrow
As it is spoke, she never will admit me.

ORSINO
Be clamorous and leap all civil bounds
Rather than make unprofited return.

VIOLA
Say I do speak with her, my lord, what then?

ORSINO
O, then unfold the passion of my love.
Surprise her with discourse of my dear faith.
It shall become thee well to act my woes.
She will attend it better in thy youth
Than in a nuncio's of more grave aspect.

VIOLA
I think not so, my lord.

ORSINO
Dear lad, believe it;
For they shall yet belie thy happy years
That say thou art a man. Diana's lip
Is not more smooth and rubious, thy small pipe
Is as the maiden's organ, shrill and sound,
And all is semblative a womans part.
I know thy constellation is right apt
For this affair.—Prosper well in this
And thou shalt live as freely as thy lord,
To call his fortunes thine.

VIOLA
I'll do my best
To woo your lady. *[Aside]* Yet a barful strife!
Whoe'er I woo, myself would be his wife.

[EXIT]

[Enter MARIA and FESTE]

MARIA
Nay, either tell me where thou hast been, or I will not open my lips so wide as a bristle may enter in way of thy excuse. My lady will hang thee for thy absence.

FESTE
Let her hang me. He that is well hanged in this world
needs to fear no colors.

MARIA
Make that good.

FESTE
He shall see none to fear.

MARIA
A good Lenten answer. I can tell thee where that saying was born,
of "I fear no colors."

FESTE
Where, good Mistress Mary?

MARIA
In the wars; and that may you be bold to say in your foolery.

FESTE
Well, God give them wisdom that have it, and
those that are Fools, let them use their talents.

MARIA
Yet you will be hanged for being so long absent.
Or to be turned away, is not that as good as a hanging to you?

FESTE
Many a good hanging prevents a bad marriage,
and, for turning away, let summer bear it out.

MARIA
You are resolute, then?

FESTE
Not so, neither, but I am resolved on two points.

MARIA
That if one break, the other will hold, or if both break, your gaskins fall.

FESTE
Apt, in good faith, very apt. Well, go thy way.
If Sir Toby would leave drinking,
thou wert as witty a piece of Eve's flesh as any in Illyria.

MARIA
Peace, you rogue. No more o' that. Here comes
my lady. Make your excuse wisely, you were best.
                    [She EXITS]

            [Enter Lady OLIVIA with MALVOLIO]

FESTE *[aside]*
Wit, an 't be thy will, put me into good fooling!
Those wits that think they have thee do very oft prove fools,
and I that am sure I lack thee may pass for a wise man.

For what says Quinapalus? "Better a witty Fool than a foolish wit."
—God bless thee, lady!

OLIVIA
Take the Fool away.

FESTE
Do you not hear, fellows? Take away the Lady.

OLIVIA
Go to, you're a dry Fool. I'll no more of you.
Besides, you grow dishonest.

FESTE
Two faults, madonna, that drink and good counsel will amend. For give the dry Fool drink, then is the Fool not dry. Bid the dishonest man mend himself; if he mend, he is no longer dishonest; if he cannot, let the botcher mend him. Anything that's mended is but patched; virtue that transgresses is but patched with sin, and sin that amends is but patched with virtue. If that this simple syllogism will serve, so; if it will not, what remedy? As there is no true cuckold but calamity, so beauty's a flower. The Lady bade take away the Fool. Therefore, I say again, take her away.

OLIVIA
Sir, I bade them take away you.

FESTE
Misprision in the highest degree! Lady, cucullus non facit monachum. That's as much to say as, I wear not motley in my brain. Good madonna, give me leave to prove you a fool.

OLIVIA
Can you do it?

FESTE
Dexteriously, good madonna.

OLIVIA
Make your proof.

FESTE
I must catechize you for it, madonna. Good my mouse of virtue, answer me.

OLIVIA
Well, sir, for want of other idleness, I'll bide your proof.

FESTE
Good madonna, why mourn'st thou?

OLIVIA
Good Fool, for my brother's death.

FESTE
I think his soul is in hell, madonna.

OLIVIA
I know his soul is in heaven, Fool.

FESTE
The more fool, madonna, to mourn for your brother's soul, being in heaven. Take away the fool, gentlemen.

OLIVIA
What think you of this Fool, Malvolio? Doth he not mend?

MALVOLIO
Yes, and shall do till the pangs of death shake him.
Infirmity, that decays the wise, doth ever make the better Fool.

FESTE
God send you, sir, a speedy infirmity, for the better increasing your folly! Sir Toby will be sworn that I am no fox, but he will not pass his word for twopence that you are no Fool.

OLIVIA
How say you to that, Malvolio?

MALVOLIO
I marvel your Ladyship takes delight in such a barren rascal. I saw him put down the other day with an ordinary Fool that has no more brain than a stone. Look you now, he's out of his guard already. Unless you laugh and minister occasion to him, he is gagged. I protest I take these wise men that crow so at these set kind of Fools no better than the Fools' zanies.

OLIVIA
O, you are sick of self-love, Malvolio, and taste with a distempered appetite. To be generous, guiltless, and of free disposition is to take those things for bird-bolts that you deem cannon bullets. There is no slander in an allowed Fool, though he do nothing but rail; nor no railing in a known discreet man, though he do nothing but reprove.

FESTE
Now Mercury endue thee with leasing, for thou speak'st well of Fools!

[Enter MARIA]

MARIA
Madam, there is at the gate a young gentleman much desires to speak with you.

OLIVIA
From the Count Orsino, is it?

MARIA
I know not, madam. 'Tis a fair young man.

OLIVIA
Who of my people hold him in delay?

MARIA
Sir Toby, madam, your kinsman.

OLIVIA
Fetch him off, I pray you. He speaks nothing but madman. Fie on him!
[MARIA exits]
Go you, Malvolio. If it be a suit from the Count, I am sick, or not at home; what you will, to dismiss it.
[MALVOLIO exits]
Now you see, sir, how your fooling grows old, and people dislike it.

FESTE
Thou hast spoke for us, madonna, as if thy eldest son should be a Fool, whose skull Jove cram with brains, for—here he comes—one of thy kin has a most weak pia mater.

[Enter Sir TOBY]

OLIVIA
By mine honor, half drunk!—What is he at the gate, cousin?

TOBY
A gentleman.

OLIVIA
A gentleman? What gentleman?

TOBY
'Tis a gentleman here—a plague o' these pickle herring!—How now, sot?

FESTE
Good Sir Toby.

OLIVIA
Cousin, cousin, how have you come so early by this lethargy?

TOBY
Lechery? I defy lechery. There's one at the gate.

OLIVIA
Ay, marry, what is he?

TOBY
Let him be the devil an he will, I care not. Give me faith, say I. Well, it's all one.
[He EXITS]

OLIVIA
What's a drunken man like, Fool?

FESTE
Like a drowned man, a fool, and a madman. One draught above heat makes him a fool, the second mads him, and a third drowns him.

OLIVIA
Go thou and seek the crowner and let him sit o' my coz, for he's in the third degree of drink: he's drowned. Go look after him.

FESTE
He is but mad yet, madonna, and the Fool shall look to the madman.
[He EXITS]
[Enter MALVOLIO]

MALVOLIO
Madam, yond young fellow swears he will speak with you. I told him you were sick; he takes on him to understand so much, and therefore comes to speak with you. I told him you were asleep; he seems to have a foreknowledge of that too, and therefore comes to speak with you. What is to be said to him, lady? He's fortified against any denial.

OLIVIA
Tell him he shall not speak with me.

MALVOLIO
Has been told so, and he says he'll stand at your door like a sheriff's post and be the supporter to a bench, but he'll speak with you.

OLIVIA
What kind o' man is he?

MALVOLIO
Why, of mankind.

OLIVIA
What manner of man?

MALVOLIO
Of very ill manner. He'll speak with you, will you or no.

OLIVIA
Of what personage and years is he?

MALVOLIO
Not yet old enough for a man, nor young enough for a boy—as a squash is before 'tis a peascod, or a codling when 'tis almost an apple. 'Tis with him in standing water, between boy and man. He is very well-favored, and he speaks very shrewishly. One would think his mother's milk were scarce out of him.

OLIVIA
Let him approach. Call in my gentlewoman.

MALVOLIO
Gentlewoman, my lady calls.
[He exits]
[Re-enter MARIA with veil]

OLIVIA
Give me my veil. Come, throw it o'er my face.
We'll once more hear Orsino's embassy.
[Enter VIOLA]

VIOLA
The honorable lady of the house, which is she?

OLIVIA
Speak to me. I shall answer for her. Your will?

VIOLA
Most radiant, exquisite, and unmatchable beauty—
I pray you, tell me if this be the lady of the house, for I never saw her. I would be loath to cast away my speech, for, besides that it is excellently well penned, I have taken great pains to con it. Good beauties, let me sustain no scorn. I am very comptible even to the least sinister usage.

OLIVIA
Whence came you, sir?

VIOLA
I can say little more than I have studied, and that question's out of my part. Good gentle one, give me modest assurance if you be the lady of the house, that I may proceed in my speech.

OLIVIA
Are you a comedian?

VIOLA
No, my profound heart. And yet by the very fangs of malice I swear I am not that I play. Are you the lady of the house?

OLIVIA
If I do not usurp myself, I am.

VIOLA
Most certain, if you are she, you do usurp yourself, for what is yours to bestow is not yours to reserve. But this is from my commission. I will on with my speech in your praise and then show you the heart of my message.

OLIVIA
Come to what is important in 't. I forgive you the praise.

VIOLA
Alas, I took great pains to study it, and 'tis poetical.

OLIVIA
It is the more like to be feigned. I pray you, keep it in. I heard you were saucy at my gates, and allowed your approach rather to wonder at you than to hear you. If you be not mad, begone; if you have reason, be brief. 'Tis not that time of moon with me to make one in so skipping a dialogue.

MARIA
Will you hoist sail, sir? Here lies your way.

VIOLA
No, good swabber, I am to hull here a little longer.—Some mollification for your giant, sweet lady.

OLIVIA
Tell me your mind.

VIOLA
I am a messenger.

OLIVIA
Sure you have some hideous matter to deliver when the courtesy of it is so fearful. Speak your office.

VIOLA
It alone concerns your ear.
I bring no overture of war, no taxation of homage.
I hold the olive in my hand.
My words are as full of peace as matter.

OLIVIA
Yet you began rudely. What are you? What would you?

VIOLA
The rudeness that hath appeared in me have I learned from my entertainment. What I am and what I would are as secret as maidenhead: to your ears, divinity; to any other's, profanation.

OLIVIA
Give us the place alone. We will hear this divinity.
                    [MARIA exit]
Now, sir, what is your text?

VIOLA
Most sweet lady—

OLIVIA
A comfortable doctrine, and much may be said of it. Where lies your text?

VIOLA
In Orsino's bosom.

OLIVIA
In his bosom? In what chapter of his bosom?

VIOLA
To answer by the method, in the first of his heart.

OLIVIA
O, I have read it; it is heresy. Have you no more to say?

VIOLA
Good madam, let me see your face.

OLIVIA
Have you any commission from your lord to negotiate with my face? You are now out of your text. But we will draw the curtain and show you the picture. *[She removes her veil]* Look you, sir, such a one I was this present. Is 't not well done?

VIOLA
Excellently done, if God did all.

OLIVIA
'Tis in grain, sir; 'twill endure wind and weather.

VIOLA
'Tis beauty truly blent, whose red and white Nature's own sweet and cunning hand laid on. Lady, you are the cruel'st she alive If you will lead these graces to the grave And leave the world no copy.

OLIVIA
O, sir, I will not be so hard-hearted! I will give out divers schedules of my beauty. It shall be inventoried and every particle and utensil labeled to my will: as, item, two lips indifferent red; item, two gray eyes with lids to them; item, one neck, one chin, and so forth. Were you sent hither to praise me?

VIOLA
I see you what you are. You are too proud.
But if you were the devil you are fair.
My lord and master loves you. O, such love
Could be but recompensed though you were crowned
The nonpareil of beauty.

OLIVIA
How does he love me?

VIOLA
With adorations, fertile tears,
With groans that thunder love, with sighs of fire.

OLIVIA
Your lord does know my mind. I cannot love him.
Yet I suppose him virtuous, know him noble,
Of great estate, of fresh and stainless youth;
In voices well divulged, free, learned, and valiant,
And in dimension and the shape of nature
A gracious person. But yet I cannot love him.
He might have took his answer long ago.

VIOLA
If I did love you in my master's flame,
With such a suff'ring, such a deadly life,
In your denial I would find no sense.
I would not understand it.

OLIVIA
Why, what would you?

VIOLA
Make me a willow cabin at your gate
And call upon my soul within the house,
Write loyal cantons of contemned love
And sing them loud even in the dead of night,
Halloo your name to the reverberate hills
And make the babbling gossip of the air
Cry out "Olivia!" O, you should not rest
Between the elements of air and earth
But you should pity me.

OLIVIA
You might do much. What is your parentage?

VIOLA
Above my fortunes, yet my state is well. I am a gentleman.

OLIVIA
Get you to your lord.
I cannot love him. Let him send no more—
Unless perchance you come to me again
To tell me how he takes it. Fare you well.
I thank you for your pains. Spend this for me.
[She offers money]

VIOLA
I am no fee'd post, lady. Keep your purse.
My master, not myself, lacks recompense.
Love make his heart of flint that you shall love,
And let your fervor, like my master's, be
Placed in contempt. Farewell, fair cruelty.
                    [She exits]

OLIVIA
"What is your parentage?" "Above my fortunes, yet my state is well.
I am a gentleman." I'll be sworn thou art.
Thy tongue, thy face, thy limbs, actions, and spirit

Do give thee fivefold blazon. Not too fast! Soft, soft!
Unless the master were the man. How now?
Even so quickly may one catch the plague?
Methinks I feel this youth's perfections
With an invisible and subtle stealth
To creep in at mine eyes. Well, let it be.—What ho, Malvolio!

[Enter MALVOLIO]

MALVOLIO
Here, madam, at your service.

OLIVIA
Run after that same peevish messenger,
The County's man. He left this ring behind him,
Would I or not. Tell him I'll none of it.
[She hands him a ring] Desire him not to flatter with his lord,
Nor hold him up with hopes. I am not for him.
If that the youth will come this way tomorrow,
I'll give him reasons for 't. Hie thee, Malvolio.

MALVOLIO
Madam, I will.

[He EXITS]

OLIVIA
I do I know not what, and fear to find
Mine eye too great a flatterer for my mind.
Fate, show thy force. Ourselves we do not owe.
What is decreed must be, and be this so.

[EXIT]

[Enter ANTONIO and SEBASTIAN]

ANTONIO
Will you stay no longer? Nor will you not that I go with you?

SEBASTIAN
By your patience, no. My stars shine darkly over me. The malignancy of my fate might perhaps distemper yours. Therefore I shall crave of you your leave that I may bear my evils alone. It were a bad recompense for your love to lay any of them on you.

ANTONIO
Let me yet know of you whither you are bound.

SEBASTIAN
No, sooth, sir. My determinate voyage is mere extravagancy. But I perceive in you so excellent a touch of modesty that you will not extort from me what I am willing to keep in. Therefore it charges me in manners the rather to express myself. You must know of me, then, Antonio, my name is Sebastian, which I called Roderigo. My father was that Sebastian of Messaline whom I know you have heard of. He left behind him myself and a sister, both born in an hour. If the heavens had been pleased, would we had so ended! But you, sir, altered that, for some hour before you took me from the breach of the sea was my sister drowned.

ANTONIO
Alas the day!

SEBASTIAN
A lady, sir, though it was said she much resembled me, was yet of many accounted beautiful. But though I could not with such estimable wonder overfar believe that, yet thus far I will boldly publish her: she bore a mind that envy could not but call fair. She is drowned already, sir, with salt water, though I seem to drown her remembrance again with more.

ANTONIO
Pardon me, sir, your bad entertainment.

SEBASTIAN
O good Antonio, forgive me your trouble.

ANTONIO
If you will not murder me for my love, let me be your servant.

SEBASTIAN
If you will not undo what you have done—that is, kill him whom you have recovered—desire it not. Fare you well at once. My bosom is full of kindness, and I am yet so near the manners of my mother that, upon the least occasion more, mine eyes will tell tales of me. I am bound to the Count Orsino's court. Farewell.
                    [He exits]

ANTONIO
The gentleness of all the gods go with thee!
I have many enemies in Orsino's court,
else would I very shortly see thee there. But come what may,
I do adore thee so that danger shall seem sport, and I will go.

                    [EXIT]

[Enter VIOLA and MALVOLIO]

MALVOLIO
Were not you even now with the Countess Olivia?

VIOLA
Even now, sir. On a moderate pace I have since arrived but hither.

MALVOLIO
She returns this ring to you, sir. You might have saved me my pains to have taken it away yourself. She adds, moreover, that you should put your lord into a desperate assurance she will none of him. And one thing more, that you be never so hardy to come again in his affairs unless it be to report your lord's taking of this. Receive it so.

VIOLA
She took the ring of me. I'll none of it.

MALVOLIO
Come, sir, you peevishly threw it to her, and her will is it should be so returned. *[He throws down the ring]* If it be worth stooping for, there it lies in your eye; if not, be it his that finds it.
[He exits]

VIOLA
I left no ring with her. What means this lady?
[She picks up the ring]
Fortune forbid my outside have not charmed her!
She made good view of me, indeed so much
That methought her eyes had lost her tongue,
For she did speak in starts distractedly.
She loves me, sure! The cunning of her passion
Invites me in this churlish messenger.
None of my lord's ring? Why, he sent her none!
I am the man. If it be so, as 'tis,
Poor lady, she were better love a dream.
How will this fadge? My master loves her dearly,
And I, poor monster, fond as much on him,
And she, mistaken, seems to dote on me.
What will become of this? As I am man,
My state is desperate for my master's love.
As I am woman (now, alas the day!),
What thriftless sighs shall poor Olivia breathe!
O Time, thou must untangle this, not I.
It is too hard a knot for me t' untie.

[EXIT]

[Enter Sir TOBY and Sir ANDREW]

TOBY
Approach, Sir Andrew. Not to be abed after midnight is to be up betimes, and "diluculo surgere," thou know'st—

ANDREW
Nay, by my troth, I know not. But I know to be up late is to be up late.

TOBY
A false conclusion. I hate it as an unfilled can. To be up after midnight and to go to bed then, is early, so that to go to bed after midnight is to go to bed betimes. Does not our lives consist of the four elements?

ANDREW
Faith, so they say, but I think it rather consists of eating and drinking.

TOBY
Thou 'rt a scholar. Let us therefore eat and drink. Marian, I say, a stoup of wine!

[Enter FESTE]

ANDREW
Here comes the Fool, i' faith.

FESTE
How now, my hearts? Did you never see the picture of "We Three"?

TOBY
Welcome, ass! Now let's have a catch.

ANDREW
By my troth, the Fool has an excellent breast. I had rather than forty shillings I had such a leg, and so sweet a breath to sing, as the Fool has.—In sooth, thou wast in very gracious fooling last night. 'Twas very good, i' faith. I sent thee sixpence for thy leman. Hadst it?

FESTE
I did impeticos thy gratillity, for Malvolio's nose is no whipstock, my lady has a white hand, and the Myrmidons are no bottle-ale houses.

ANDREW
Excellent! Why, this is the best fooling when all is done. Now, a song!

TOBY *[giving money]*
Come on, there is sixpence for you. Let's have a song.

ANDREW
[giving money] There's a testril of me, too. If one knight give a—

FESTE
Would you have a love song or a song of good life?

TOBY
A love song, a love song.

ANDREW
Ay, ay, I care not for good life.

FESTE *[sings]*
O mistress mine, where are you roaming?
O mistress mine, where are you roaming?
O, stay and hear! Your truelove's coming,
That can sing both high and low.
Trip no further, pretty sweeting.
Journeys end in lovers meeting,
Every wise man's son doth know.

What is love? 'Tis not hereafter.
What is love? 'Tis not hereafter.
Present mirth hath present laughter.
What's to come is still unsure.
In delay there lies no plenty,
Then come kiss me, sweet and twenty.
Youth's a stuff will not endure.

ANDREW
A mellifluous voice, as I am true knight.

TOBY
A contagious breath.

ANDREW
Very sweet and contagious, i' faith.

TOBY
To hear by the nose, it is dulcet in contagion. But shall we make the welkin dance indeed? Shall we rouse the night owl in a catch that will draw three souls out of one weaver? Shall we do that?

ANDREW
An you love me, let's do 't. I am dog at a catch.

FESTE
By 'r Lady, sir, and some dogs will catch well.

ANDREW
Most certain. Let our catch be "Thou Knave."

FESTE
"Hold thy peace, thou knave," knight? I shall be constrained in 't to call thee "knave," knight.

ANDREW
'Tis not the first time I have constrained one to call me "knave." Begin, Fool. It begins "Hold thy peace."

FESTE
I shall never begin if I hold my peace.

ANDREW
Good, i' faith. Come, begin.
[Catch sung]

[Enter MARIA]

MARIA
What a caterwauling do you keep here! If my lady have not called up her steward Malvolio and bid him turn you out of doors, never trust me.

TOBY
My lady's a Cataian, we are politicians, Malvolio's a Peg-a-Ramsey, and *[Sings]* Three merry men be we.
Am not I consanguineous? Am I not of her blood? Tillyvally! "Lady"!
[Sings] There dwelt a man in Babylon, lady, lady.

FESTE
Beshrew me, the knight's in admirable fooling.

ANDREW
Ay, he does well enough if he be disposed, and so do I, too. He does it with a better grace, but I do it more natural.

TOBY *[sings]*
O' the twelfth day of December—

MARIA
For the love o' God, peace!

[Enter MALVOLIO]

MALVOLIO
My masters, are you mad? Or what are you? Have you no wit, manners, nor honesty but to gabble like tinkers at this time of night? Do you make an ale-house of my lady's house, that you squeak out your coziers' catches without any mitigation or remorse of voice? Is there no respect of place, persons, nor time in you?

TOBY
We did keep time, sir, in our catches. Sneck up!

MALVOLIO
Sir Toby, I must be round with you. My lady bade me tell you that, though she harbors you as her kinsman, she's nothing allied to your disorders. If you can separate yourself and your misdemeanors, you are welcome to the house; if not, an it would please you to take leave of her, she is very willing to bid you farewell.

TOBY *[sings]*
Farewell, dear heart, since I must needs be gone.

MARIA
Nay, good Sir Toby.

FESTE *[sings]*
His eyes do show his days are almost done.

MALVOLIO
Is 't even so?

TOBY *[sings]*
But I will never die.

FESTE *[sings]*
Sir Toby, there you lie.

MALVOLIO
This is much credit to you.

TOBY *[sings]*
Shall I bid him go?

FESTE *[sings]*
What an if you do?

TOBY *[sings]*
Shall I bid him go, and spare not?

FESTE *[sings]*
O no, no, no, no, you dare not.

TOBY
Out o' tune, sir? You lie. Art any more than a steward? Dost thou think, because thou art virtuous, there shall be no more cakes and ale?

FESTE
Yes, by Saint Anne, and ginger shall be hot i' th' mouth, too.

TOBY
Thou 'rt i' th' right.—Go, sir, rub your chain with crumbs.—A stoup of wine, Maria!

MALVOLIO
Mistress Mary, if you prized my lady's favor at anything more than contempt, you would not give means for this uncivil rule. She shall know of it, by this hand.
[He exits]

MARIA
Go shake your ears!

ANDREW
'Twere as good a deed as to drink when a man's a-hungry,
to challenge him the field and then to break promise with him
and make a fool of him.

TOBY
Do 't, knight. I'll write thee a challenge.
Or I'll deliver thy indignation to him by word of mouth.

MARIA
Sweet Sir Toby, be patient for tonight. Since the youth of the Count's was today with my lady, she is much out of quiet. For Monsieur Malvolio, let me alone with him. If I do not gull him into a nayword and make him a common recreation, do not think I have wit enough to lie straight in my bed. I know I can do it.

TOBY
Possess us, possess us, tell us something of him.

MARIA
Marry, sir, sometimes he is a kind of puritan.

ANDREW
O, if I thought that, I'd beat him like a dog!

TOBY
What, for being a puritan? Thy exquisite reason, dear knight?

ANDREW
I have no exquisite reason for 't, but I have reason good enough.

MARIA
The devil a puritan that he is, or anything constantly but a time-pleaser; an affectioned ass that cons state without book and utters it by great swaths; the best persuaded of himself, so crammed, as he thinks, with excellencies, that it is his grounds of faith that all that look on him love him. And on that vice in him will my revenge find notable cause to work.

TOBY
What wilt thou do?

MARIA
I will drop in his way some obscure epistles of love, wherein by the color of his beard, the shape of his leg, the manner of his gait, the expressure of his eye, forehead, and complexion, he shall find himself most feelingly personated. I can write very like my lady your niece; on a forgotten matter, we can hardly make distinction of our hands.

TOBY
Excellent! I smell a device.

ANDREW
I have 't in my nose, too.

TOBY
He shall think, by the letters that thou wilt drop, that they come from my niece, and that she's in love with him.

MARIA
My purpose is indeed a horse of that color.

ANDREW
And your horse now would make him an ass.

MARIA
Ass, I doubt not.

ANDREW
O, 'twill be admirable!

MARIA
Sport royal, I warrant you. I know my physic will work with him. I will plant you two, and let the Fool make a third, where he shall find the letter. Observe his construction of it. For this night, to bed, and dream on the event. Farewell.

TOBY
Good night, Penthesilea.

[She exits]

ANDREW
Before me, she's a good wench.

TOBY
She's a beagle true bred, and one that adores me. What o' that?

ANDREW
I was adored once, too.

TOBY
Let's to bed, knight. Thou hadst need send for more money.

ANDREW
If I cannot recover your niece, I am a foul way out.

TOBY
Send for money, knight. If thou hast her not i' th' end, call me "Cut."

ANDREW
If I do not, never trust me, take it how you will.

TOBY
Come, come, I'll go burn some sack. 'Tis too late to go to bed now. Come, knight; come, knight.

[EXIT]

[Enter ORSINO, VIOLA, and VALENTINE]

ORSINO
Give me some music. *[Music plays]* Now, good morrow, friends.—
Now, good Cesario, but that piece of song,

That old and antique song we heard last night.
Methought it did relieve my passion much,
More than light airs and recollected terms
Of these most brisk and giddy-paced times.
Come, but one verse.

VALENTINE
He is not here, so please your Lordship, that should sing it.

ORSINO
Who was it?

VALENTINE
Feste the jester, my lord, a Fool that the Lady Olivia took much delight in. He is about the house.

ORSINO
Seek him out
               [VALENTINE exits]
and play the tune the while. *[Music plays offstage]*
[To Viola] Come hither, boy. If ever thou shalt love,
In the sweet pangs of it remember me,
For such as I am, all true lovers are,
Unstaid and skittish in all motions else
Save in the constant image of the creature
That is beloved. How dost thou like this tune?

VIOLA
It gives a very echo to the seat
Where love is throned.

ORSINO
Thou dost speak masterly.
My life upon 't, young though thou art, thine eye
Hath stayed upon some favor that it loves.
Hath it not, boy?

VIOLA
A little, by your favor.

ORSINO
What kind of woman is 't?

VIOLA
Of your complexion.

ORSINO
She is not worth thee, then. What years, i' faith?

VIOLA
About your years, my lord.

ORSINO
Too old, by heaven. Let still the woman take an elder than herself. So wears she to him; So sways she level in her husband's heart. For, boy, however we do praise ourselves. Our fancies are more giddy and unfirm, more longing, wavering, sooner lost and worn, than women's are.

VIOLA
I think it well, my lord.

ORSINO
Then let thy love be younger than thyself,
Or thy affection cannot hold the bent.
For women are as roses, whose fair flower,
Being once displayed, doth fall that very hour.

VIOLA
And so they are. Alas, that they are so,
To die even when they to perfection grow!

[Enter VALENTINE and FESTE]

ORSINO
O, fellow, come, the song we had last night.—Mark it, Cesario. It is old and plain; It is silly sooth, and dallies with the innocence of love Like the old age.

FESTE
Are you ready, sir?

ORSINO
Ay, prithee, sing.

FESTE *[sings]*
Come away, come away, death,
And in sad cypress let me be laid.
Fly away, fly away, breath,
I am slain by a fair cruel maid.

A thousand thousand sighs to save,
Lay me, O, where
Sad true lover never find my grave
To weep there.

ORSINO *[giving money]*
There's for thy pains.

FESTE
No pains, sir. I take pleasure in singing, sir.

ORSINO
I'll pay thy pleasure, then.

FESTE
Truly sir, and pleasure will be paid, one time or another.

ORSINO
Give me now leave to leave thee.

FESTE
Now the melancholy god protect thee and the tailor make thy doublet of changeable taffeta, for thy mind is a very opal. I would have men of such constancy put to sea, that their business might be everything and their intent everywhere, for that's it that always makes a good voyage of nothing. Farewell.
[FESTE exits]

ORSINO
Let all the rest give place.
[VALENTINE and all but ORSINO and VIOLA exit]
Once more, Cesario,
Get thee to yond same sovereign cruelty.
Tell her my love, more noble than the world,
Prizes not quantity of dirty lands.
The parts that Fortune hath bestowed upon her,
Tell her, I hold as giddily as Fortune.
But 'tis that miracle and queen of gems
That nature pranks her in attracts my soul.

VIOLA
But if she cannot love you, sir—

ORSINO
I cannot be so answered.

VIOLA
Sooth, but you must. Say that some lady, as perhaps there is,
Hath for your love as great a pang of heart
As you have for Olivia. You cannot love her;
You tell her so. Must she not then be answered?

ORSINO
There is no woman's sides can bide the beating of so strong a passion as love doth give my heart; no woman's heart so big, to hold so much. Make no compare between that love a woman can bear me and
that I owe Olivia.

VIOLA
Ay, but I know—

ORSINO
What dost thou know?

VIOLA
Too well what love women to men may owe. In faith, they are as true of heart as we. My father had a daughter loved a man as it might be, perhaps, were I a woman, I should your Lordship.

ORSINO
And what's her history?

VIOLA
A blank, my lord. She never told her love,
But let concealment, like a worm i' th' bud,
Feed on her damask cheek. She pined in thought,
And with a green and yellow melancholy
She sat like Patience on a monument,
Smiling at grief. Was not this love indeed?
We men may say more, swear more, but indeed
Our shows are more than will; for still we prove
Much in our vows but little in our love.

ORSINO
But died thy sister of her love, my boy?

VIOLA
I am all the daughters of my father's house,
And all the brothers, too—and yet I know not.
Sir, shall I to this lady?

ORSINO
Ay, that's the theme. To her in haste. Give her this jewel.
Say my love can give no place, bide no denay.
[He hands her a jewel]

[EXIT]

[Enter Sir TOBY, Sir ANDREW, and FABIAN]

TOBY
Come thy ways, Signior Fabian.

FABIAN
Nay, I'll come. If I lose a scruple of this sport, let me be boiled to death with melancholy.

TOBY
Wouldst thou not be glad to have the rascally sheep-biter come by some notable shame?

FABIAN
I would exult, man. You know he brought me out o' favor with my lady about a bearbaiting here.

TOBY
To anger him, we'll have the bear again, and we will fool him black and blue, shall we not, Sir Andrew?

ANDREW An we do not, it is pity of our lives.

[Enter MARIA]

TOBY
Here comes the little villain.—How now, my metal of India?

MARIA
Get you all three into the boxtree. Malvolio's coming down this walk. He has been yonder i' the sun practicing behavior to his own shadow this half hour. Observe him, for the love of mockery, for I know this letter will make a contemplative idiot of him. Close, in the name of jesting! *[They hide]* Lie thou there *[putting down the letter]*
for here comes the trout that must be caught with tickling.
[She exits]

[Enter MALVOLIO]

MALVOLIO
'Tis but fortune, all is fortune. Maria once told me she did affect me, and I have heard herself come thus near, that should she fancy, it should be one of my complexion. Besides, she uses me with a more exalted respect than anyone else that follows her. What should I think on 't?

TOBY *[aside]*
Here's an overweening rogue.

FABIAN *[aside]*
O, peace! Contemplation makes a rare turkeycock of him.
How he jets under his advanced plumes!

ANDREW *[aside]*
'Slight, I could so beat the rogue!

TOBY *[aside]*
Peace, I say.

MALVOLIO
To be Count Malvolio.

TOBY *[aside]*
Ah, rogue!

ANDREW *[aside]*
Pistol him, pistol him!

TOBY *[aside]*
Peace, peace!

MALVOLIO
There is example for 't. The lady of the
Strachy married the yeoman of the wardrobe.

ANDREW *[aside]*
Fie on him, Jezebel!

FABIAN *[aside]*
O, peace, now he's deeply in. Look how imagination blows him.

MALVOLIO
Having been three months married to her, sitting in my state—

TOBY *[aside]*
O, for a stone-bow, to hit him in the eye!

MALVOLIO
Calling my officers about me, in my branched velvet gown, having come
from a daybed where I have left Olivia sleeping—

TOBY *[aside]*
Fire and brimstone!

FABIAN [aside]
O, peace, peace!

MALVOLIO
And then to have the humor of state; and after a demure travel of regard, telling them I know my place, as I would they should do theirs, to ask for my kinsman Toby—

TOBY [aside]
Bolts and shackles!

FABIAN [aside]
O, peace, peace, peace! Now, now.

MALVOLIO
Seven of my people, with an obedient start, make out for him. I frown the while, and perchance wind up my watch, or play with my—some rich jewel. Toby approaches; curtsies there to me—

TOBY [aside]
Shall this fellow live?

FABIAN [aside]
Though our silence be drawn from us with cars, yet peace!

MALVOLIO
I extend my hand to him thus, quenching my familiar smile with an austere regard of control—

TOBY [aside]
And does not Toby take you a blow o' the lips then?

MALVOLIO
Saying, "Cousin Toby, my fortunes, having cast me on your niece, give me this prerogative of speech—"

TOBY [aside]
What, what?

MALVOLIO
"You must amend your drunkenness."

TOBY [aside]
Out, scab!

FABIAN *[aside]*
Nay, patience, or we break the sinews of our plot!

MALVOLIO
"Besides, you waste the treasure of your time with a foolish knight—"

ANDREW *[aside]*
That's me, I warrant you.

MALVOLIO
"One Sir Andrew."

ANDREW *[aside]*
I knew 'twas I, for many do call me fool.

MALVOLIO *[seeing the letter]*
What employment have we here?

FABIAN *[aside]*
Now is the woodcock near the gin.

TOBY *[aside]*
O, peace, and the spirit of humors intimate reading aloud to him.

MALVOLIO *[taking up the letter]*
By my life, this is my lady's hand! These be her very c's, her u's, and her t's, and thus she makes her great P's. It is in contempt of question her hand.

ANDREW *[aside]*
Her c's, her u's, and her t's. Why that?

MALVOLIO
[reads] To the unknown beloved, this, and my good wishes—Her very phrases! By your leave, wax. Soft. And the impressure her Lucrece, with which she uses to seal—'tis my lady! *[He opens the letter]*
To whom should this be?

FABIAN *[aside]*
This wins him, liver and all.

MALVOLIO [reads]
Jove knows I love,
But who?
Lips, do not move;
No man must know.

"No man must know." What follows? The numbers altered.
"No man must know." If this should be thee, Malvolio!

TOBY [aside]
Marry, hang thee, brock!

MALVOLIO [reads]
I may command where I adore,
But silence, like a Lucrece knife,
With bloodless stroke my heart doth gore;
M.O.A.I. doth sway my life.

FABIAN [aside]
A fustian riddle!

TOBY [aside]
Excellent wench, say I.

MALVOLIO
"M.O.A.I. doth sway my life." Nay, but first let me see, let me see, let me see.

FABIAN [aside]
What dish o' poison has she dressed him!

TOBY [aside]
And with what wing the staniel checks at it!

MALVOLIO
"I may command where I adore." Why, she may command me; I serve her; she is my lady. Why, this is evident to any formal capacity. There is no obstruction in this. And the end—what should that alphabetical position portend? If I could make that resemble something in me! Softly! "M.O.A.I."—
"M"—Malvolio. "M"—why, that begins my name!
"M." But then there is no consonancy in the sequel that suffers under probation. "A" should follow, but "O" does.

FABIAN [aside]
And "O" shall end, I hope.

TOBY [aside]
Ay, or I'll cudgel him and make him cry "O."

MALVOLIO
And then "I" comes behind.

FABIAN *[aside]*
Ay, an you had any eye behind you, you might see more detraction at your heels than fortunes before you.

MALVOLIO
"M.O.A.I." This simulation is not as the former, and yet to crush this a little, it would bow to me, for every one of these letters are in my name. Soft, here follows prose.

[He reads] If this fall into thy hand, revolve. In my stars I am above thee, but be not afraid of greatness. Some are born great, some achieve greatness, and some have greatness thrust upon 'em. Thy fates open their hands. Cast thy humble slough and appear fresh. Be opposite with a kinsman, surly with servants. Let thy tongue tang arguments of state. Put thyself into the trick of singularity. She thus advises thee that sighs for thee. Remember who commended thy yellow stockings and wished to see thee ever cross-gartered. I say, remember. Go to, thou art made, if thou desir'st to be so. If not, let me see thee a steward still, the fellow of servants, and not worthy to touch Fortune's fingers. Farewell. She that would alter services with thee, The Fortunate-Unhappy.

Daylight and champian discovers not more! This is open. I will be proud, I will read politic authors, I will baffle Sir Toby, I will wash off gross acquaintance, I will be point-devise the very man. I do not now fool myself, to let imagination jade me; for every reason excites to this, that my lady loves me. She did commend my yellow stockings of late, she did praise my leg being cross-gartered, and in this she manifests herself to my love and, with a kind of injunction, drives me to these habits of her liking. I thank my stars, I am happy. I will be strange, stout, in yellow stockings, and cross-gartered, even with the swiftness of putting on. Jove and my stars be praised! Here is yet a postscript.

[He reads] Thou canst not choose but know who I am.
If thou entertain'st my love, let it appear in thy smiling;
thy smiles become thee well. Therefore in my presence still smile,
dear my sweet, I prithee.

Jove, I thank thee! I will smile. I will do everything that thou wilt have me.
[He exits]

FABIAN
I will not give my part of this sport for a pension of thousands to be paid from the Sophy.

TOBY
I could marry this wench for this device.

ANDREW
So could I too.

TOBY
And ask no other dowry with her but such another jest.

ANDREW
Nor I neither.

[Enter MARIA]

FABIAN
Here comes my noble gull-catcher.

TOBY
Wilt thou set thy foot o' my neck?

ANDREW
Or o' mine either?

TOBY
Shall I play my freedom at tray-trip and become thy bondslave?

ANDREW
I' faith, or I either?

TOBY
Why, thou hast put him in such a dream that when the image of it leaves him he must run mad.

MARIA
Nay, but say true, does it work upon him?

TOBY
Like aqua vitae with a midwife.

MARIA
If you will then see the fruits of the sport, mark his first approach before my lady. He will come to her in yellow stockings, and 'tis a color she abhors, and cross-gartered, a fashion she detests; and he will smile upon her, which will now be so unsuitable to her disposition, being addicted to a melancholy as she is, that it cannot but turn him into a notable contempt. If you will see it, follow me.

TOBY
To the gates of Tartar, thou most excellent devil of wit!

ANDREW
I'll make one, too.

[EXIT]

ACT 2

[Enter VIOLA and FESTE]

VIOLA
Save thee, friend, and thy music. Dost thou live by thy tabor?

FESTE
No, sir, I live by the church.

VIOLA
Art thou a churchman?

FESTE
No such matter, sir. I do live by the church, for I do live at my house, and my house doth stand by the church.

VIOLA
So thou mayst say the king lies by a beggar if a beggar dwell near him, or the church stands by thy tabor if thy tabor stand by the church.

FESTE
You have said, sir. To see this age! A sentence is but a chev'ril glove to a good wit. How quickly the wrong side may be turned outward!

VIOLA
Nay, that's certain. I warrant thou art a merry fellow and car'st for nothing.

FESTE
Not so, sir. I do care for something. But in my conscience, sir,
I do not care for you. If that be to care for nothing, sir,
I would it would make you invisible.

VIOLA
Art not thou the Lady Olivia's Fool?

FESTE
No, indeed, sir. The Lady Olivia has no folly. She will keep no Fool, sir, till she be married, and Fools are as like husbands as pilchers are to herrings: the husband's the bigger. I am indeed not her Fool but her corrupter of words.

VIOLA
I saw thee late at the Count Orsino's.

FESTE
Foolery, sir, does walk about the orb like the sun; it shines everywhere.
I would be sorry, sir, but the Fool should be as oft with your master as
with my mistress. I think I saw your Wisdom there.

VIOLA
Nay, an thou pass upon me, I'll no more with thee.
Hold, there's expenses for thee. *[Giving a coin]*

FESTE
Now Jove, in his next commodity of hair, send thee a beard!

VIOLA
By my troth I'll tell thee, I am almost sick for one *[aside]* though I would
not have it grow on my chin.—Is thy lady within?

FESTE
Would not a pair of these have bred, sir?

VIOLA
Yes, being kept together and put to use.

FESTE
I would play Lord Pandarus of Phrygia, sir, to bring a
Cressida to this Troilus.

VIOLA
I understand you, sir. 'Tis well begged. *[Giving another coin]*

FESTE
The matter I hope is not great, sir, begging but a beggar: Cressida was a
beggar. My lady is within, sir. I will conster to them whence you come.
Who you are and what you would are out of my welkin—I might say
"element," but the word is overworn.
[He exits]

VIOLA
This fellow is wise enough to play the Fool, And to do that well craves a
kind of wit. He must observe their mood on whom he jests,
The quality of persons, and the time, And, like the haggard, check at
every feather That comes before his eye.

[Enter Sir TOBY and ANDREW]

TOBY
Save you, gentleman.

VIOLA
And you, sir.

ANDREW
Dieu vous garde, monsieur.

VIOLA
Et vous aussi. Votre serviteur!

ANDREW
I hope, sir, you are, and I am yours.

TOBY
Will you encounter the house?
My niece is desirous you should enter, if your trade be to her.

VIOLA
I am bound to your niece, sir; I mean, she is the list of my voyage.

TOBY
Taste your legs, sir; put them to motion.

VIOLA
My legs do better understand me, sir,
than I understand what you mean by bidding me taste my legs.

TOBY
I mean, to go, sir, to enter.

VIOLA
I will answer you with gait and entrance—but we are prevented.

[Enter OLIVIA and MARIA]

Most excellent accomplished lady, the heavens rain odors on you!

ANDREW *[aside]*
That youth's a rare courtier. "Rain odors," well.

VIOLA
My matter hath no voice, lady, but to your own most pregnant and vouchsafed ear.

ANDREW *[aside]*
"Odors," "pregnant," and "vouchsafed." I'll get 'em all three all ready.

OLIVIA

Let the garden door be shut, and leave me to my hearing.
            [Sir TOBY, Sir ANDREW, and MARIA exit]
Give me your hand, sir.

VIOLA

My duty, madam, and most humble service.

OLIVIA

What is your name?

VIOLA

Cesario is your servant's name, fair princess.

OLIVIA

My servant, sir? 'Twas never merry world
Since lowly feigning was called compliment.
You're servant to the Count Orsino, youth.

VIOLA

And he is yours, and his must needs be yours.
Your servant's servant is your servant, madam.

OLIVIA

For him, I think not on him. For his thoughts,
Would they were blanks rather than filled with me.

VIOLA

Madam, I come to whet your gentle thoughts
On his behalf.

OLIVIA

O, by your leave, I pray you.
I bade you never speak again of him.
But would you undertake another suit,
I had rather hear you to solicit that
Than music from the spheres.

VIOLA

Dear lady—

OLIVIA

Give me leave, beseech you. I did send,
After the last enchantment you did here,
A ring in chase of you. So did I abuse
Myself, my servant, and, I fear me, you. What might you think?

Have you not set mine honor at the stake
And baited it with all th' unmuzzled thoughts
That tyrannous heart can think? To one of your receiving
Enough is shown. A cypress, not a bosom,
Hides my heart. So, let me hear you speak.

VIOLA
I pity you.

OLIVIA
That's a degree to love.

VIOLA
No, not a grize, for 'tis a vulgar proof
That very oft we pity enemies.

OLIVIA
Why then methinks 'tis time to smile again.
O world, how apt the poor are to be proud!
                    [Clock strikes]
Be not afraid, good youth, I will not have you.
And yet when wit and youth is come to harvest,
Your wife is like to reap a proper man.
There lies your way, due west.

VIOLA
Then westward ho!
Grace and good disposition attend your Ladyship.
You'll nothing, madam, to my lord by me?

OLIVIA
Stay. I prithee, tell me what thou think'st of me.

VIOLA
That you do think you are not what you are.

OLIVIA
If I think so, I think the same of you.

VIOLA
Then think you right. I am not what I am.

OLIVIA
I would you were as I would have you be.

VIOLA
Would it be better, madam, than I am?
I wish it might, for now I am your fool.

OLIVIA *[aside]*
O, what a deal of scorn looks beautiful
In the contempt and anger of his lip!
Cesario, by the roses of the spring,
By maidhood, honor, truth, and everything,
I love thee so, that, maugre all thy pride,
Nor wit nor reason can my passion hide.
Do not extort thy reasons from this clause,
For that I woo, thou therefore hast no cause;
But rather reason thus with reason fetter:
Love sought is good, but given unsought is better.

VIOLA
By innocence I swear, and by my youth,
I have one heart, one bosom, and one truth,
And that no woman has, nor never none
Shall mistress be of it, save I alone.
And so adieu, good madam. Nevermore
Will I my master's tears to you deplore.

OLIVIA
Yet come again, for thou perhaps mayst move
That heart, which now abhors, to like his love.

[They EXIT in different directions]

[Enter Sir TOBY, Sir ANDREW, and FABIAN]

ANDREW
No, faith, I'll not stay a jot longer.

TOBY
Thy reason, dear venom, give thy reason.

FABIAN
You must needs yield your reason, Sir Andrew.

ANDREW
Marry, I saw your niece do more favors to the Count's servingman than ever she bestowed upon me. I saw 't i' th' orchard.

TOBY
Did she see thee the while, old boy? Tell me that.

ANDREW
As plain as I see you now.

FABIAN
This was a great argument of love in her toward you.

ANDREW
'Slight, will you make an ass o' me?

FABIAN
I will prove it legitimate, sir, upon the oaths of judgment and reason. She did show favor to the youth in your sight only to exasperate you, to awake your dormouse valor. You should have banged the youth into dumbness.

TOBY
Challenge me the Count's youth to fight with him. Hurt him in eleven places. My niece shall take note of it.

FABIAN
There is no way but this, Sir Andrew.

ANDREW
Will either of you bear me a challenge to him?

TOBY
Go, write it in a martial hand. Be curst and brief. It is no matter how witty, so it be eloquent and full of invention. Taunt him with the license of ink. Let there be gall enough in thy ink, though thou write with a goose-pen, no matter. About it.

ANDREW
Where shall I find you?

TOBY
We'll call thee at the cubiculo. Go.

[Sir ANDREW exits]

FABIAN
This is a dear manikin to you, Sir Toby.

TOBY
I have been dear to him, lad, some two thousand strong or so.

FABIAN
We shall have a rare letter from him. But you'll not deliver 't?

TOBY
Never trust me, then. And by all means stir on the youth to an answer. For Andrew, if he were opened and you find so much blood in his liver as will clog the foot of a flea, I'll eat the rest of th' anatomy.

FABIAN
And his opposite, the youth, bears in his visage
no great presage of cruelty.

[Enter MARIA]

TOBY
Look where the youngest wren of mine comes.

MARIA
If you desire the spleen, and will laugh yourselves into stitches, follow me. Yond gull Malvolio is turned heathen, a very renegado; for there is no Christian that means to be saved by believing rightly can ever believe such impossible passages of grossness. He's in yellow stockings.

TOBY
And cross-gartered?

MARIA
Most villainously, like a pedant that keeps a school i' th' church. I have dogged him like his murderer. He does obey every point of the letter that I dropped to betray him. He does smile his face into more lines than is in the new map with the augmentation of the Indies. You have not seen such a thing as 'tis. I know my lady will strike him. If she do, he'll smile and take 't for a great favor.

TOBY
Come, bring us, bring us where he is.

[EXIT]

[Enter SEBASTIAN and ANTONIO]

SEBASTIAN
I would not by my will have troubled you,
But, since you make your pleasure of your pains,
I will no further chide you.

ANTONIO
I could not stay behind you. My desire,
More sharp than filed steel, did spur me forth;
And not all love to see you.

SEBASTIAN
My kind Antonio, I can no other answer make but thanks,
And thanks, and ever thanks; and oft good turns
Are shuffled off with such uncurrent pay.
But were my worth, as is my conscience, firm,
You should find better dealing. What's to do?
Shall we go see the relics of this town?

ANTONIO
Tomorrow, sir. Best first go see your lodging.

SEBASTIAN
I am not weary, and 'tis long to night.
I pray you, let us satisfy our eyes
With the memorials and the things of fame
That do renown this city.

ANTONIO
Would you'd pardon me.
I do not without danger walk these streets.
Once in a sea fight 'gainst the Count his galleys
I did some service, of such note indeed
That were I ta'en here it would scarce be answered.

SEBASTIAN
Do not then walk too open.

ANTONIO
It doth not fit me. Hold, sir, here's my purse.
[Giving him money] In the south suburbs, at the Elephant,
Is best to lodge. I will bespeak our diet
Whiles you beguile the time and feed your knowledge
With viewing of the town. There shall you have me.

SEBASTIAN
Why I your purse?

ANTONIO
Haply your eye shall light upon some toy
You have desire to purchase, and your store,
I think, is not for idle markets, sir.

SEBASTIAN
I'll be your purse-bearer and leave you
For an hour.

ANTONIO
To th' Elephant.

SEBASTIAN
I do remember.
[They EXIT in different directions]

[Enter OLIVIA and MARIA]

OLIVIA [aside]
I have sent after him. He says he'll come. How shall I feast him? What bestow of him? For youth is bought more oft than begged or borrowed. I speak too loud.— Where's Malvolio? He is sad and civil and suits well for a servant with my fortunes. Where is Malvolio?

MARIA
He's coming, madam, but in very strange manner.
He is sure possessed, madam.

OLIVIA
Why, what's the matter? Does he rave?

MARIA
No, madam, he does nothing but smile. Your Ladyship were best to have some guard about you if he come, for sure the man is tainted in 's wits.

OLIVIA
Go call him hither. *[MARIA exits]*

I am as mad as he, If sad and merry madness equal be.

[Enter MARIA with MALVOLIO]

How now, Malvolio?

MALVOLIO
Sweet lady, ho, ho!

OLIVIA
Smil'st thou? I sent for thee upon a sad occasion.

MALVOLIO
Sad, lady? I could be sad. This does make some obstruction in the blood, this cross-gartering, but what of that? If it please the eye of one, it is with me as the very true sonnet is: "Please one, and please all."

OLIVIA
Why, how dost thou, man? What is the matter with thee?

MALVOLIO
Not black in my mind, though yellow in my legs.
It did come to his hands, and commands shall be executed.
I think we do know the sweet Roman hand.

OLIVIA
Wilt thou go to bed, Malvolio?

MALVOLIO
To bed? "Ay, sweetheart, and I'll come to thee."

OLIVIA
God comfort thee! Why dost thou smile so, and kiss thy hand so oft?

MARIA
How do you, Malvolio?

MALVOLIO
At your request? Yes, nightingales answer daws!

MARIA
Why appear you with this ridiculous boldness before my lady?
[MARIA exits]

MALVOLIO
"Be not afraid of greatness." 'Twas well writ.

OLIVIA
What mean'st thou by that, Malvolio?

MALVOLIO
"Some are born great—"

OLIVIA
Ha?

MALVOLIO
"Some achieve greatness—"

OLIVIA
What sayst thou?

MALVOLIO
"And some have greatness thrust upon them."

OLIVIA
Heaven restore thee!

MALVOLIO
"Remember who commended thy yellow stockings—"

OLIVIA
Thy yellow stockings?

MALVOLIO
"And wished to see thee cross-gartered."

OLIVIA
Cross-gartered?

MALVOLIO
"Go to, thou art made, if thou desir'st to be so—"

OLIVIA
Am I made?

MALVOLIO
"If not, let me see thee a servant still."

OLIVIA
Why, this is very midsummer madness!

[Enter MARIA]

MARIA
Madam, the young gentleman of the Count Orsino's is returned.
I could hardly entreat him back.
He attends your Ladyship's pleasure.

OLIVIA
I'll come to him. Good Maria, let this fellow be looked to. Where's my Cousin Toby? Let some of my people have a special care of him. I would not have him miscarry for the half of my dowry.

[OLIVIA and MARIA exit in different directions]

MALVOLIO
O ho, do you come near me now? No worse man than Sir Toby to look to me. This concurs directly with the letter. She sends him on purpose that I may appear stubborn to him, for she incites me to that in the letter: "Cast thy humble slough," says she. "Be opposite with a kinsman, surly with servants; let thy tongue tang with arguments of state; put thyself into the trick of singularity," and consequently sets down the manner how: as, a sad face, a reverend carriage. And when she went away now, "Let this fellow be looked to." "Fellow!" Not "Malvolio," nor after my degree, but "fellow." Why, everything adheres together, that no dram of a scruple, no scruple of a scruple, no obstacle, no incredulous or unsafe circumstance—what can be said? Nothing that can be can come between me and the full prospect of my hopes. Well, Jove, not I, is the doer of this, and he is to be thanked.

[Enter TOBY, FABIAN, and MARIA]

TOBY
Which way is he, in the name of sanctity? If all the devils of hell be drawn in little, and Legion himself possessed him, yet I'll speak to him.

FABIAN
Here he is, here he is.—How is 't with you, sir? How is 't with you, man?

MALVOLIO
Go off, I discard you. Let me enjoy my private. Go off.

MARIA *[to Toby]*
Lo, how hollow the fiend speaks within him! Did not I tell you? Sir Toby, my lady prays you to have a care of him.

MALVOLIO
Aha, does she so?

TOBY [to Fabian and Maria]
Go to, go to! Peace, peace. We must deal gently with him. Let me alone.—How do you, Malvolio? How is 't with you? What, man, defy the devil! Consider, he's an enemy to mankind.

MALVOLIO
Do you know what you say?

MARIA *[to Toby]*
La you, an you speak ill of the devil, how he takes it at heart! Pray God he be not bewitched!

FABIAN
Carry his water to th' wisewoman.

MARIA
Marry, and it shall be done tomorrow morning if I live.
My lady would not lose him for more than I'll say.

MALVOLIO
How now, mistress?

MARIA
O Lord!

TOBY
Prithee, hold thy peace. This is not the way.
Do you not see you move him? Let me alone with him.

FABIAN
No way but gentleness, gently, gently.
The fiend is rough and will not be roughly used.

TOBY *[to Malvolio]*
Why, how now, my bawcock? How dost thou, chuck?

MALVOLIO
Sir!

MARIA
Get him to say his prayers, good Sir Toby; get him to pray.

MALVOLIO
My prayers, minx?

MARIA *[to Toby]*
No, I warrant you, he will not hear of godliness.

MALVOLIO
Go hang yourselves all! You are idle, shallow things. I am not of your element. You shall know more hereafter.

[He EXITS]

TOBY
Is 't possible?

FABIAN
If this were played upon a stage now, I could condemn it as an improbable fiction.

MARIA
Nay, pursue him now, lest the device take air and taint.

FABIAN
Why, we shall make him mad indeed.

MARIA
The house will be the quieter.

TOBY
Come, we'll have him in a dark room and bound. My niece is already in the belief that he's mad. But see, but see!

[Enter Sir ANDREW]

FABIAN
More matter for a May morning.

ANDREW *[presenting a paper]*
Here's the challenge. Read it. I warrant there's vinegar and pepper in 't.

FABIAN
Is 't so saucy?

ANDREW
Ay, is 't. I warrant him. Do but read.

TOBY
Give me. *[reads]* Youth, whatsoever thou art, thou art but a scurvy fellow.

FABIAN
Good, and valiant.

TOBY *[reads]*
Wonder not nor admire not in thy mind why I do call thee so, for I will show thee no reason for 't.

FABIAN
A good note, that keeps you from the blow of the law.

TOBY *[reads]*
Thou com'st to the Lady Olivia, and in my sight she uses thee kindly. But thou liest in thy throat; that is not the matter I challenge thee for.

FABIAN
Very brief, and to exceeding good sense—less.

TOBY *[reads]* I will waylay thee going home, where if it be
thy chance to kill me—

FABIAN
Good.

TOBY *[reads]*
Thou kill'st me like a rogue and a villain.

FABIAN
Still you keep o' th' windy side of the law. Good.

TOBY *[reads]* Fare thee well, and God have mercy upon
one of our souls. He may have mercy upon mine, but
my hope is better, and so look to thyself. Thy friend, as
thou usest him, and thy sworn enemy, Andrew Aguecheek.
If this letter move him not, his legs cannot. I'll give 't him.

MARIA
You may have very fit occasion for 't.
He is now in some commerce with my lady
and will by and by depart.

TOBY
Go, Sir Andrew. So soon as ever thou seest him,
draw, and as thou draw'st, swear horrible. Away!

ANDREW
Nay, let me alone for swearing.

[He EXITS]

TOBY
Now will not I deliver his letter.
But, sir, I will deliver his challenge by word of mouth,
set upon Aguecheek a notable report of valor,
and drive the gentleman (as I know his youth will aptly receive it)
into a most hideous opinion of his rage, skill, fury, and impetuosity.
This will so fright them both that they will kill one another
by the look, like cockatrices.

[Enter OLIVIA and VIOLA]

FABIAN
Here he comes with your niece. Give them
way till he take leave, and presently after him.

TOBY
I will meditate the while upon some horrid
message for a challenge.

[TOBY, FABIAN, and MARIA exit]

OLIVIA
I have said too much unto a heart of stone and laid mine honor too
unchary on 't. There's something in me that reproves my fault, But such a
headstrong potent fault it is that it but mocks reproof.

VIOLA
With the same 'havior that your passion bears
Goes on my master's griefs.

OLIVIA
Here, wear this jewel for me. 'Tis my picture.
Refuse it not. It hath no tongue to vex you.
And I beseech you come again tomorrow.
What shall you ask of me that I'll deny,
That honor, saved, may upon asking give?

VIOLA
Nothing but this: your true love for my master.

OLIVIA
How with mine honor may I give him that
Which I have given to you?

VIOLA
I will acquit you.

OLIVIA
Well, come again tomorrow. Fare thee well.
A fiend like thee might bear my soul to hell.
[She exits]

[Enter TOBY and FABIAN]

TOBY
Gentleman, God save thee.

VIOLA
And you, sir.

TOBY
That defense thou hast, betake thee to 't.
Thy intercepter, full of despite, bloody as the hunter,
attends thee at the orchard end. Thy assailant is quick,
skillful, and deadly.

VIOLA
You mistake, sir. I am sure no man hath any quarrel to me.
My remembrance is very free and clear from any image of
offense done to any man.

TOBY
You'll find it otherwise, I assure you. Therefore, if you hold your life at
any price, betake you to your guard.

VIOLA
I pray you, sir, what is he?

TOBY
He is knight dubbed with unhatched rapier and on carpet consideration,
but he is a devil in private brawl. Souls and bodies hath he divorced
three, and satisfaction can be none but by pangs of death and sepulcher.
"Hob, nob" is his word; "give 't or take 't."

VIOLA
I will return again into the house and desire some conduct of the lady.
I am no fighter. I have heard of some kind of men that put quarrels
purposely on others to taste their valor. Belike this is a man of that quirk.

TOBY
Sir, no. His indignation derives itself out of a very competent injury.
Therefore get you on and give him his desire.
Back you shall not to the house.

VIOLA
This is as uncivil as strange. I beseech you, do me this courteous office,
as to know of the knight what my offense to him is. It is something of my
negligence, nothing of my purpose.

TOBY
I will do so.—Signior Fabian, stay you by this gentleman till my return.
[TOBY exits]

VIOLA
Pray you, sir, do you know of this matter?

FABIAN
I know the knight is incensed against you even to a mortal arbitrament, but nothing of the circumstance more.

VIOLA
I beseech you, what manner of man is he?

FABIAN
He is indeed, sir, the most skillful, bloody, and fatal opposite that you could possibly have found in any part of Illyria. Will you walk towards him? I will make your peace with him if I can.

VIOLA
I shall be much bound to you for 't. I am one that had rather go with Sir Priest than Sir Knight, I care not who knows so much of my mettle.
[EXIT]
[Enter TOBY and ANDREW]

TOBY
Why, man, he's a very devil. I have not seen such a firago. I had a pass with him, rapier, scabbard, and all, and he gives me the stuck-in with such a mortal motion that it is inevitable.

ANDREW
Pox on 't! I'll not meddle with him.

TOBY
Ay, but he will not now be pacified. Fabian can scarce hold him yonder.

ANDREW
Plague on 't! An I thought he had been valiant, and so cunning in fence, I'd have seen him damned ere I'd have challenged him. Let him let the matter slip, and I'll give him my horse, gray Capilet.

TOBY
I'll make the motion. Stand here, make a good show on 't. This shall end without the perdition of souls.
[Enter FABIAN and VIOLA]
[TOBY crosses to meet them]

TOBY *[to Viola]*
There's no remedy, sir; he will fight with you for 's oath sake.

VIOLA
Pray God defend me! *[Aside]* A little thing would make me tell them how much I lack of a man.

FABIAN
Give ground if you see him furious.
> *[TOBY crosses to ANDREW]*

TOBY
Come, Sir Andrew, there's no remedy. The gentleman will, for his honor's sake, have one bout with you. He cannot by the duello avoid it. But he has promised me, as he is a gentleman and a soldier, he will not hurt you. Come on, to 't.

ANDREW *[drawing his sword]*
Pray God he keep his oath!

VIOLA *[drawing her sword]*
I do assure you 'tis against my will.

> *[Enter ANTONIO]*

ANTONIO *[to Andrew]*
Put up your sword. If this young gentleman
Have done offense, I take the fault on me.
If you offend him, I for him defy you.

TOBY
You, sir? Why, what are you?

ANTONIO *[drawing his sword]*
One, sir, that for his love dares yet do more
Than you have heard him brag to you he will.

TOBY *[drawing his sword]*
Nay, if you be an undertaker, I am for you.

> *[Enter OFFICER]*

FABIAN
O, good Sir Toby, hold! Here comes the officer.

TOBY *[to Antonio]*
I'll be with you anon.

VIOLA *[to Andrew]*
Pray, sir, put your sword up, if you please.

ANDREW
Marry, will I, sir. And for that I promised you,
I'll be as good as my word.

OFFICER
Antonio, I arrest thee at the suit of Count Orsino.

ANTONIO
You do mistake me, sir.

OFFICER
No, sir, no jot. I know your favor well,
Though now you have no sea-cap on your head.—
Take him away. He knows I know him well.

ANTONIO
I must obey. *[To Viola]* This comes with seeking you.
But there's no remedy. I shall answer it.
What will you do, now my necessity
Makes me to ask you for my purse? It grieves me
Much more for what I cannot do for you
Than what befalls myself. You stand amazed,
But be of comfort.

OFFICER
Come, sir, away.

ANTONIO *[to Viola]*
I must entreat of you some of that money.

VIOLA
What money, sir? For the fair kindness you have showed me here,
And part being prompted by your present trouble,
Out of my lean and low ability I'll lend you something.
Hold, there's half my coffer.
                    [Offering him money]

ANTONIO
Will you deny me now?
Is 't possible that my deserts to you
Can lack persuasion? Do not tempt my misery,
Lest that it make me so unsound a man
As to upbraid you with those kindnesses
That I have done for you.

VIOLA
I know of none, nor know I you by voice or any feature.

ANTONIO
O heavens themselves!

OFFICER
Come, sir, I pray you go.

ANTONIO
Let me speak a little. This youth that you see here
I snatched one half out of the jaws of death,
Relieved him with such sanctity of love,
And to his image, which methought did promise
Most venerable worth, did I devotion.

OFFICER
What's that to me? The time goes by. Away!

ANTONIO
But O, how vile an idol proves this god!
Thou hast, Sebastian, done good feature shame.
In nature there's no blemish but the mind;
None can be called deformed but the unkind.

OFFICER
The man grows mad. Away with him.—Come, come, sir.

ANTONIO
Lead me on.
                    [ANTONIO and OFFICER exit]

VIOLA *[aside]*
Methinks his words do from such passion fly that he believes himself;
so do not I. Prove true, imagination, O, prove true, that I, dear brother,
be now ta'en for you!

TOBY
Come hither, knight; come hither, Fabian. We'll
whisper o'er a couplet or two of most sage saws.

            [TOBY, FABIAN, and ANDREW move aside]

VIOLA *[aside]*
He named Sebastian. I my brother know
Yet living in my glass. Even such and so
In favor was my brother, and he went
Still in this fashion, color, ornament,
For him I imitate. O, if it prove,
Tempests are kind, and salt waves fresh in love!

                    [She EXITS]

TOBY
A very dishonest, paltry boy, and more a coward than a hare. His dishonesty appears in leaving his friend here in necessity and denying him; and for his cowardship, ask Fabian.

FABIAN
A coward, a most devout coward, religious in it.

ANDREW
'Slid, I'll after him again and beat him.

TOBY
Do, cuff him soundly, but never draw thy sword.

ANDREW
An I do not—

FABIAN
Come, let's see the event.

TOBY
I dare lay any money 'twill be nothing yet.

[EXIT]

[Enter SEBASTIAN and FESTE]

FESTE
Will you make me believe that I am not sent for you?

SEBASTIAN
Go to, go to, thou art a foolish fellow. Let me be clear of thee.

FESTE
Well held out, i' faith. No, I do not know you, nor I am not sent to you by my lady to bid you come speak with her, nor your name is not Master Cesario, nor this is not my nose neither. Nothing that is so is so.

SEBASTIAN
I prithee, vent thy folly somewhere else. Thou know'st not me.

FESTE
Vent my folly? He has heard that word of some great man and now applies it to a Fool. Vent my folly? I prithee now, ungird thy strangeness and tell me what I shall vent to my lady. Shall I vent to her that thou art coming?

SEBASTIAN
I prithee, foolish Greek, depart from me. There's money for thee.
[Giving money] If you tarry longer, I shall give worse payment.

FESTE
By my troth, thou hast an open hand. These wise men that give Fools money get themselves a good report—after fourteen years' purchase.

[Enter ANDREW, TOBY, and FABIAN]

ANDREW *[to Sebastian]*
Now, sir, have I met you again? There's for you.

[He strikes SEBASTIAN]

SEBASTIAN *[returning the blow]*
Why, there's for thee, and there, and there.—Are all the people mad?

TOBY
Hold, sir, or I'll throw your dagger o'er the house.

FESTE *[aside]*
This will I tell my lady straight.
I would not be in some of your coats for twopence.
[He EXITS]

TOBY *[seizing Sebastian]*
Come on, sir, hold!

ANDREW
Nay, let him alone. I'll go another way to work with him. I'll have an action of battery against him, if there be any law in Illyria. Though I struck him first, yet it's no matter for that.

SEBASTIAN *[to Toby]*
Let go thy hand!

TOBY
Come, sir, I will not let you go. Come, my young soldier, put up your iron. Come on.

SEBASTIAN
I will be free from thee. What wouldst thou now?
If thou dar'st tempt me further, draw thy sword.

TOBY
What, what? Nay, then, I must have an ounce or two of this malapert blood from you.

[Enter Olivia]

OLIVIA
Hold, Toby! On thy life I charge thee, hold!

TOBY
Madam.

OLIVIA
Will it be ever thus? Ungracious wretch,
Fit for the mountains and the barbarous caves,
Where manners ne'er were preached! Out of my sight!—
Be not offended, dear Cesario.— Rudesby, begone!

[TOBY, ANDREW, and FABIAN exit]

I prithee, gentle friend,
Let thy fair wisdom, not thy passion, sway
In this uncivil and unjust extent
Against thy peace. Go with me to my house,
And hear thou there how many fruitless pranks
This ruffian hath botched up, that thou thereby
Mayst smile at this. Thou shalt not choose but go.
Do not deny. Beshrew his soul for me!
He started one poor heart of mine, in thee.

SEBASTIAN *[aside]*
What relish is in this? How runs the stream?
Or I am mad, or else this is a dream.
Let fancy still my sense in Lethe steep;
If it be thus to dream, still let me sleep!

OLIVIA
Nay, come, I prithee. Would thou 'dst be ruled by me!

SEBASTIAN
Madam, I will.

OLIVIA
O, say so, and so be!

[EXIT]

[Enter MARIA and FESTE]

MARIA
Nay, I prithee, put on this gown and this beard; make him believe thou art Sir Topas the curate. Do it quickly. I'll call Sir Toby the whilst.
[She EXITS]

FESTE
Well, I'll put it on and I will dissemble myself in 't, and I would I were the first that ever dissembled in such a gown. I am not tall enough to become the function well, nor lean enough to be thought a good student, but to be said an honest man and a good housekeeper goes as fairly as to say a careful man and a great scholar. The competitors enter.

[Enter TOBY and MARIA]

TOBY
Jove bless thee, Master Parson.

FESTE
Bonos dies, Sir Toby;

TOBY
To him, Sir Topas.

FESTE *[disguising his voice]*
What ho, I say! Peace in this prison!

TOBY
The knave counterfeits well. A good knave.

MALVOLIO *[within]*
Who calls there?

FESTE
Sir Topas the curate, who comes to visit Malvolio the lunatic.

MALVOLIO
Sir Topas, Sir Topas, good Sir Topas, go to my lady—

FESTE
Out, hyperbolical fiend! How vexest thou this man! Talkest thou nothing but of ladies?

TOBY *[aside]*
Well said, Master Parson.

MALVOLIO
Sir Topas, never was man thus wronged. Good Sir Topas,
do not think I am mad. They have laid me here in hideous darkness—

FESTE
Fie, sayst thou that house is dark?

MALVOLIO
As hell, Sir Topas.

FESTE
Why, it hath bay windows transparent as barricadoes, and the clerestories
toward the south-north are as lustrous as ebony; and yet complainest
thou of obstruction?

MALVOLIO
I am not mad, Sir Topas. I say to you this house is dark.

FESTE
Madman, thou errest. I say there is no darkness but ignorance.

MALVOLIO
I say this house is as dark as ignorance, though ignorance
were as dark as hell. And I say there was never man thus abused.
I am no more mad than you are.

FESTE
Fare thee well. Remain thou still in darkness.

MALVOLIO
Sir Topas, Sir Topas!

TOBY
My most exquisite Sir Topas!

MARIA
Thou mightst have done this without thy beard and gown.
He sees thee not.

TOBY
To him in thine own voice, and bring me word how thou find'st him.
I would we were well rid of this knavery.
Come by and by to my chamber.

[TOBY and MARIA exit]

FESTE [sings]
Hey, Robin, jolly Robin, tell me how thy lady does.

MALVOLIO
Fool!

FESTE [sings]
My lady is unkind, perdy.

MALVOLIO
Fool!

FESTE [sings]
Alas, why is she so?

MALVOLIO
Fool, I say!

FESTE [sings]
She loves another— Who calls, ha?

MALVOLIO
Good fool, as ever thou wilt deserve well at my hand,
help me to a candle, and pen, ink, and paper.
As I am a gentleman, I will live to be thankful to thee for 't.

FESTE
Master Malvolio?

MALVOLIO
Ay, good Fool.

FESTE
Alas, sir, how fell you besides your five wits?

MALVOLIO
Fool, there was never man so notoriously
abused. I am as well in my wits, Fool, as thou art.

FESTE
But as well? Then you are mad indeed,
if you be no better in your wits than a Fool.

MALVOLIO
They have here propertied me, keep me in darkness, send ministers to
me—asses!—and do all they can to face me out of my wits.

FESTE
Advise you what you say. The minister is here.
[In the voice of Sir Topas] Malvolio, Malvolio, thy wits the heavens restore. Endeavor thyself to sleep and leave thy vain bibble-babble.

MALVOLIO
Sir Topas!

FESTE *[as Sir Topas]*
Maintain no words with him, good fellow.
[As Fool] Who, I, sir? Not I, sir! God buy you, good Sir Topas.
[As Sir Topas] Marry, amen.
[As Fool] I will, sir, I will.

MALVOLIO
Fool! Fool! Fool, I say! Good Fool, help me to some light and some paper. I tell thee, I am as well in my wits as any man in Illyria.

FESTE
Welladay that you were, sir!

MALVOLIO
By this hand, I am. Good Fool, some ink, paper, and light; and convey what I will set down to my lady.

FESTE
I will help you to 't. But tell me true, are you not mad indeed, or do you but counterfeit?

MALVOLIO
Believe me, I am not. I tell thee true.

FESTE
I will fetch you light and paper and ink.

MALVOLIO
Fool, I'll requite it in the highest degree. I prithee, begone.

FESTE *[sings]*
I am gone, sir, and anon, sir,
I'll be with you again,
In a trice, like to the old Vice,
Your need to sustain...
                    [EXIT]

[Enter SEBASTIAN]

SEBASTIAN
This is the air; that is the glorious sun.
This pearl she gave me, I do feel 't and see 't.
And though 'tis wonder that enwraps me thus,
Yet 'tis not madness. Where's Antonio, then?
I could not find him at the Elephant.
Yet there he was; and there I found this credit,
That he did range the town to seek me out.
His counsel now might do me golden service.
For though my soul disputes well with my sense
That this may be some error, but no madness,
That I am ready to distrust mine eyes
And wrangle with my reason that persuades me
To any other trust but that I am mad—
Or else the lady's mad. Yet if 'twere so,
She could not sway her house, command her followers,
Take and give back affairs and their dispatch
With such a smooth, discreet, and stable bearing
As I perceive she does. There's something in 't
That is deceivable. But here the lady comes.

[Enter OLIVIA and PRIEST]

OLIVIA *[to Sebastian]*
Blame not this haste of mine. If you mean well,
Now go with me and with this holy man
Into the chantry by. There, before him
And underneath that consecrated roof,
Plight me the full assurance of your faith,
That my most jealous and too doubtful soul
May live at peace. What do you say?

SEBASTIAN
I'll follow this good man and go with you,
And, having sworn truth, ever will be true.

OLIVIA
Then lead the way, good father, and heavens so shine
That they may fairly note this act of mine.

[EXIT]

[Enter FESTE and FABIAN]

FABIAN
Now, as thou lov'st me, let me see his letter.

FESTE
Good Master Fabian, grant me another request.

FABIAN
Anything.

FESTE
Do not desire to see this letter.

FABIAN
This is to give a dog and in recompense desire my dog again.

[Enter ORSINO, VIOLA, and CURIO]

ORSINO
Belong you to the Lady Olivia, friends?

FESTE
Ay, sir, we are some of her trappings.

ORSINO
I know thee well. How dost thou, my good fellow?

FESTE
Truly, sir, the better for my foes and the worse for my friends.

ORSINO
Just the contrary: the better for thy friends.

FESTE
No, sir, the worse.

ORSINO
How can that be?

FESTE
Marry, sir, they praise me and make an ass of me. Now my foes tell me plainly I am an ass; so that by my foes, sir, I profit in the knowledge of myself, and by my friends I am abused. So that, conclusions to be as kisses, if your four negatives make your two affirmatives, why then the worse for my friends and the better for my foes.

ORSINO
Why, this is excellent.

FESTE
By my troth, sir, no—though it please you to be one of my friends.

ORSINO [giving a coin]
Thou shalt not be the worse for me; there's gold.

FESTE
But that it would be double-dealing, sir, I would you could make it another.

ORSINO
O, you give me ill counsel.

FESTE
Put your grace in your pocket, sir, for this once, and let your flesh and blood obey it.

ORSINO
Well, I will be so much a sinner to be a double-dealer: there's another.
[He gives a coin]

FESTE
Primo, secundo, tertio is a good play, and the old saying is, the third pays for all. The triplex, sir, is a good tripping measure, or the bells of Saint Bennet, sir, may put you in mind—one, two, three.

ORSINO
You can fool no more money out of me at this throw. If you will let your lady know I am here to speak with her, and bring her along with you, it may awake my bounty further.

FESTE
Marry, sir, let your bounty take a nap. I will awake it anon.
[He EXITS]
[Enter ANTONIO and OFFICER]

VIOLA
Here comes the man, sir, that did rescue me.

ORSINO
That face of his I do remember well. Yet when I saw it last, it was besmeared in the smoke of war. What's the matter?

OFFICER
Orsino, this is that Antonio
That took the Phoenix and her fraught from Candy,
Here in the streets, desperate of shame and state,
In private brabble did we apprehend him.

VIOLA
He did me kindness, sir, drew on my side,
But in conclusion put strange speech upon me.
I know not what 'twas but distraction.

ORSINO
Notable pirate, thou saltwater thief,
What foolish boldness brought thee to their mercies
Whom thou, in terms so bloody and so dear,
Hast made thine enemies?

ANTONIO
Orsino, noble sir,
Be pleased that I shake off these names you give me.
Antonio never yet was thief or pirate,
Though, I confess, on base and ground enough,
Orsino's enemy. A witchcraft drew me hither.
That most ingrateful boy there by your side
From the rude sea's enraged and foamy mouth
Did I redeem; a wrack past hope he was.
His life I gave him. For his sake
Did I expose myself, pure for his love,
Into the danger of this adverse town;
Drew to defend him when he was beset;
Where, being apprehended, his false cunning
Taught him to face me out of his acquaintance;
denied me mine own purse,
Which I had recommended to his use
Not half an hour before.

VIOLA
How can this be?

ORSINO [to ANTONIO] When came he to this town?

ANTONIO
Today, my lord; and for three months before,
No int'rim, not a minute's vacancy,
Both day and night did we keep company.

[Enter OLIVIA and ATTENDANT]

ORSINO
Here comes the Countess. Now heaven walks on Earth!—
But for thee, fellow: fellow, thy words are madness.
Three months this youth hath tended upon me—
But more of that anon. *[To OFFICER]* Take him aside.

OLIVIA
What would my lord, but that he may not have,
Wherein Olivia may seem serviceable?—
Cesario, you do not keep promise with me.

VIOLA
Madam?

ORSINO
Gracious Olivia—

OLIVIA
What do you say, Cesario?—Good my lord—

VIOLA
My lord would speak; my duty hushes me.

OLIVIA
If it be aught to the old tune, my lord,
It is as fat and fulsome to mine ear
As howling after music.

ORSINO
Still so cruel?

OLIVIA
Still so constant, lord.

ORSINO
What, to perverseness? You, uncivil lady—what shall I do?

OLIVIA
Even what it please my lord that shall become him.

ORSINO
Why should I not, had I the heart to do it,
Like to the Egyptian thief, at point of death, kill what I love?
A savage jealousy that sometimes savours nobly.

Then hear me this: Since you to nonregardance cast my faith,
And that I partly know the instrument
That screws me from my true place in your favor,
Live you the marble-breasted tyrant still.
But this your minion, whom I know you love,
And whom, by heaven I swear, I tender dearly,
Him will I tear out of that cruel eye
Where he sits crowned in his master's spite.—
Come, boy, with me. My thoughts are ripe in mischief.
I'll sacrifice the lamb that I do love
To spite a raven's heart within a dove.

VIOLA
And I, most jocund, apt, and willingly,
To do you rest a thousand deaths would die.

OLIVIA
Where goes Cesario?

VIOLA
After him I love more than I love these eyes, more than my life,
More by all mores than e'er I shall love wife.

OLIVIA
Ay me, detested! How am I beguiled!

VIOLA
Who does beguile you? Who does do you wrong?

OLIVIA
Hast thou forgot thyself? Is it so long?—
Call forth the holy father.
                        [ATTENDANT exits]

ORSINO *[to Viola]*
Come, away!

OLIVIA
Whither, my lord?—Cesario, husband, stay.

ORSINO
Husband?

OLIVIA
Ay, husband. Can he that deny?

ORSINO
Her husband, sirrah?

VIOLA
No, my lord, not I.

[Enter PRIEST]

OLIVIA
O, welcome, father. Father, I charge thee by thy reverence here to unfold what thou dost know hath newly passed between this youth and me.

PRIEST
A contract of eternal bond of love,
Confirmed by mutual joinder of your hands,
Attested by the holy close of lips,
Strengthened by interchangement of your rings,
And all the ceremony of this compact
Sealed in my function, by my testimony;

ORSINO *[to Viola]*
O thou dissembling cub! What wilt thou be
When time hath sowed a grizzle on thy case?
Or will not else thy craft so quickly grow
That thine own trip shall be thine overthrow?
Farewell, and take her, but direct thy feet
Where thou and I henceforth may never meet.

VIOLA
My lord, I do protest—

OLIVIA
O, do not swear.
Hold little faith, though thou hast too much fear.

[Enter Sir ANDREW]

ANDREW
For the love of God, a surgeon! Send one presently to Sir Toby.

OLIVIA
What's the matter?

ANDREW
He has broke my head across, and has given Sir Toby a bloody coxcomb too. For the love of God, your help!

OLIVIA
Who has done this, Sir Andrew?

ANDREW
The Count's gentleman, one Cesario. We took him for a coward, but he's the very devil incardinate.

ORSINO
My gentleman Cesario?

ANDREW
'Od's lifelings, here he is!—You broke my head for nothing, and that that I did, I was set on to do 't by Sir Toby.

VIOLA
Why do you speak to me? I never hurt you.
You drew your sword upon me without cause,
But I bespake you fair and hurt you not.

ANDREW
If a bloody coxcomb be a hurt, you have hurt me.
I think you set nothing by a bloody coxcomb.

[Enter TOBY and FESTE]

Here comes Sir Toby halting. You shall hear more.

ORSINO
How now, gentleman? How is 't with you?

TOBY
That's all one. Has hurt me, and there's th' end on 't.
[To FESTE] Sot, didst see Dick Surgeon, sot?

FESTE
O, he's drunk, Sir Toby, an hour agone;
his eyes were set at eight i' th' morning.

TOBY
Then he's a rogue; I hate a drunken rogue.

OLIVIA
Away with him! Who hath made this havoc with them?

ANDREW
I'll help you, Sir Toby, because we'll be dressed together.

TOBY
Will you help?—an ass-head, and a coxcomb, and a knave, a thin-faced knave, a gull?

OLIVIA
Get him to bed, and let his hurt be looked to.

[TOBY, ANDREW, FESTE, and FABIAN exit]

[Enter SEBASTIAN]

SEBASTIAN
I am sorry, madam, I have hurt your kinsman,
But, had it been the brother of my blood,
I must have done no less with wit and safety.
You throw a strange regard upon me, and by that
I do perceive it hath offended you.
Pardon me, sweet one, even for the vows
We made each other but so late ago.

ORSINO
One face, one voice, one habit, and two persons!
A natural perspective, that is and is not!

SEBASTIAN
Antonio, O, my dear Antonio! How have the hours racked and tortured me since I have lost thee!

ANTONIO
Sebastian are you?

SEBASTIAN
Fear'st thou that, Antonio?

ANTONIO
How have you made division of yourself? An apple cleft in two is not more twin than these two creatures. Which is Sebastian?

OLIVIA
Most wonderful!

SEBASTIAN *[looking at Viola]*
Do I stand there? I never had a brother. I had a sister whom the blind waves and surges have devoured. Of charity, what kin are you to me? What countryman? What name? What parentage?

VIOLA
Of Messaline. Sebastian was my father. Such a Sebastian was my brother too. So went he suited to his watery tomb. If spirits can assume both form and suit, You come to fright us.

SEBASTIAN
A spirit I am indeed, but am in that dimension grossly clad
Which from the womb I did participate.
Were you a woman, as the rest goes even,
I should my tears let fall upon your cheek
And say "Thrice welcome, drowned Viola."

VIOLA
My father had a mole upon his brow.

SEBASTIAN
And so had mine.

VIOLA
And died that day when Viola from her birth
Had numbered thirteen years.

SEBASTIAN
O, that record is lively in my soul!
He finished indeed his mortal act
That day that made my sister thirteen years.

VIOLA
If nothing lets to make us happy both
But this my masculine usurped attire,
Do not embrace again till circumstance
Of place, time, fortune, do cohere and jump
That I am Viola; which to confirm,
I'll bring you to a captain in this town,
Where lie my maiden weeds; by whose gentle help
I was preserved to serve this noble count.
All the occurrence of my fortune since
Hath been between this lady and this lord.

SEBASTIAN *[to Olivia]*
So comes it, lady, you have been mistook.
You would have been contracted to a maid.
Nor are you therein, by my life, deceived:
You are betrothed both to a maid and man.

ORSINO [to Olivia]
Be not amazed; right noble is his blood.
If this be so, as yet the glass seems true,
I shall have share in this most happy wrack.—
Boy, thou hast said to me a thousand times
Thou never shouldst love woman like to me.

VIOLA
And all those sayings will I overswear,
And all those swearings keep as true in soul
As doth that orbed continent the fire
That severs day from night.

ORSINO
Give me thy hand, and let me see thee in thy woman's weeds.

VIOLA
The Captain that did bring me first on shore hath my maid's garments.

[Enter FESTE and FABIAN]

Olivia
Fetch Malvolio hither. And yet, alas, now I remember me,
They say, poor gentleman, he's much distract. How does he, sirrah?

FESTE
He has here writ a letter to you. I should have given 't you today morning.

OLIVIA
Open 't and read it.

FESTE
Look then to be well edified, when the Fool delivers the madman.
[reads] By the Lord, madam, you wrong me, and the world shall know it.
Though you have put me into darkness and given your drunken cousin
rule over me, yet have I the benefit of my senses as well as your Ladyship.
I have your own letter that induced me to the semblance I put on.
Think of me as you please. I leave my duty a little unthought of and
speak out of my injury.
The madly used Malvolio.

OLIVIA
Did he write this?

FESTE
Ay, madam.

ORSINO
This savors not much of distraction.

OLIVIA
See him delivered, Fabian. Bring him hither.
                    [FABIAN exits]
[To ORSINO] My lord, so please you, these things further thought on,
To think me as well a sister as a wife,
One day shall crown th' alliance on 't, so please you,
Here at my house, and at my proper cost.

ORSINO
Madam, I am most apt t' embrace your offer.
[To Viola] Your master quits you; and for your service done him,
So much against the mettle of your sex,
So far beneath your soft and tender breeding,
And since you called me "master" for so long,
Here is my hand. You shall from this time be
Your master's mistress.

OLIVIA [to Viola] A sister! You are she.
            [Enter MALVOLIO and FABIA]

ORSINO
Is this the madman?

OLIVIA
Ay, my lord, this same.—How now, Malvolio?

MALVOLIO
Madam, you have done me wrong, Notorious wrong.

OLIVIA
Have I, Malvolio? No.

MALVOLIO [handing her a paper]
Lady, you have. Pray you peruse that letter.
You must not now deny it is your hand.
Write from it if you can, in hand or phrase,
Or say 'tis not your seal, not your invention.
You can say none of this. Well, grant it then,
And tell me, in the modesty of honor,
Why you have given me such clear lights of favor?
Bade me come smiling and cross-gartered to you,
To put on yellow stockings, and to frown
Upon Sir Toby and the lighter people?

And, acting this in an obedient hope,
Why have you suffered me to be imprisoned,
Kept in a dark house, visited by the priest,
And made the most notorious geck and gull
That e'er invention played on? Tell me why.

OLIVIA
Alas, Malvolio, this is not my writing,
Though I confess much like the character.
But out of question, 'tis Maria's hand.
And now I do bethink me, it was she
First told me thou wast mad; then cam'st in smiling,
And in such forms which here were presupposed
Upon thee in the letter.

FABIAN
Good madam, hear me speak,
Most freely I confess, myself and Toby
Set this device against Malvolio here,
Upon some stubborn and uncourteous parts
We had conceived against him. Maria writ
The letter at Sir Toby's great importance,
In recompense whereof he hath married her.

OLIVIA *[to Malvolio]*
Alas, poor fool, how have they baffled thee!

FESTE
Why, "some are born great, some achieve greatness,
and some have greatness thrust upon them."
And thus the whirligig of time brings in his revenges.

MALVOLIO
I'll be revenged on the whole pack of you!

[He EXITS]

OLIVIA
He hath been most notoriously abused.

ORSINO
Pursue him and entreat him to a peace.

[EXIT all but ORSINO, VIOLA, and FOOL]

Meantime, Cesario, come,
For so you shall be while you are a man.
But when in other habits you are seen,
Orsino's mistress, and his fancy's queen.

[All but the FOOL exit]

FESTE *[sings]*
When that I was and a little tiny boy,
With hey, ho, the wind and the rain,
A foolish thing was but a toy,
For the rain it raineth every day.

But when I came to man's estate,
With hey, ho, the wind and the rain,
'Gainst knaves and thieves men shut their gate,
For the rain it raineth every day.

A great while ago the world begun,
With hey, ho, the wind and the rain,
But that's all one, our play is done,
And we'll strive to please you every day.

[EXIT]

Feste's Song
The Wind & The Rain

Arr. by Lou Okell

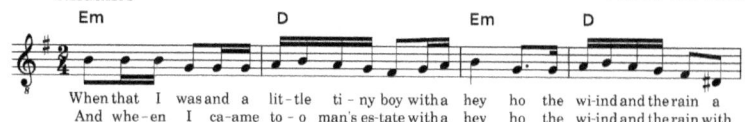

When that I was and a lit-tle ti-ny boy with a hey ho the wi-ind and the rain a
And whe-en I ca-ame to-o man's es-tate with a hey ho the wi-ind and the rain with
A long time a-go the wo-orld be-e-gun with a hey ho the wi-ind and the rain Now

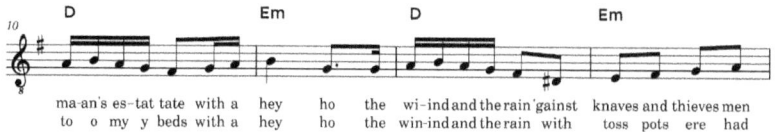

fool-ish thing was bu-ut a-a toy and the rain it rain-eth ev-er-y-y day And when I-I came to-o
swag-gering could I no-ot sur-r-vive and the rain it rain-eth ev-er-y-y day And when I I came un-n
that's all done our pla-ay i-is done and we aim to please you ev-er-y-y day!

ma-an's es-tat tate with a hey ho the wi-ind and the rain 'gainst knaves and thieves men
to o my y beds with a hey ho the win-ind and the rain with toss pots ere had

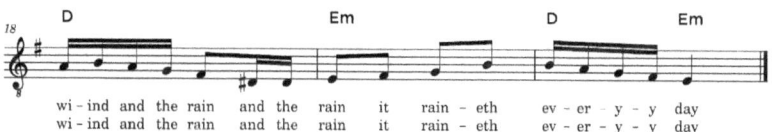

shu-ut the-eir gates and the rain it rain-eth ev-er-y-y day with a hey ho the
dru-unk e-en heads and the rain it rain-eth ev-er-y-y day with a hey ho the

wi-ind and the rain and the rain it rain-eth ev-er-y-y day
wi-ind and the rain and the rain it rain-eth ev-er-y-y day

Favorite Monologues
by William Shakespeare
adapted by Jane Farnol

Notes on performing a night of monologues

The monologues listed are selected to provide a wide range of opportunities for contemporary performers to explore Shakespeare's work. Some are challenging and others more accessible. The selection also includes a wide range of "types" for young and old, male and female, and a variety of approaches. The order was carefully selected to create an evening that will be entertaining and have a pace that will keep audiences engaged.

Favorite Monologues

CHARACTER	PLAY	PAGE
Jacques	*As You Like It*	98
Portia	*The Merchant Of Venice*	99
Hamlet	*Hamlet*	100
Trinculo	*The Tempest*	101
Claudius	*Hamlet*	102-103
Falstaff	*Merry Wives of Windsor*	104
Aaron	*Titus Andronicus*	105
Ophelia	*Hamlet*	106-107
Macbeth	*Macbeth*	108
Nurse	*Romeo & Juliet*	109
Chorus	*Henry V*	110-112
Isabella	*Measure For Measure*	113
Orsino	*Twelfth Night*	114-115
Phebe	*As You Like It*	116
Shylock	*The Merchant Of Venice*	117
Richard	*Richard III*	118-119
Gertrude	*Hamlet*	120
Henry	*Henry V*	121
Jailor's Daughter	*Two Nobel Kinsmen*	122-123
Enobarbus	*Antony & Cleopatra*	124-125
Viola	*Twelfth Night*	126
Joan la Pucelle	*Henry VI Pt. 1*	127
Malvolio	*Twelth Night*	128-131
Queen Margaret	*Henry VI Pt. 3*	132-133
First Fairy	*A Midsummer Night's Dream*	134-135
Hamlet	*Hamlet*	136-138
Richard	*Richard II*	139-140
Rosalind	*As You Like It*	141

As You Like It

Act 2 Scene 7

JACQUES

All the world's a stage,
And all the men and women merely players.
They have their exits and their entrances,
And one man in his time plays many parts,
His acts being seven ages. At first the infant,
Mewling and puking in the nurse's arms.
Then the whining schoolboy with his satchel
And shining morning face, creeping like snail
Unwillingly to school. And then the lover,
Sighing like furnace, with a woeful ballad
Made to his mistress' eyebrow. Then a soldier,
Full of strange oaths and bearded like the pard,
Jealous in honor, sudden and quick in quarrel,
Seeking the bubble reputation
Even in the cannon's mouth. And then the justice,
In fair round belly with good capon lined,
With eyes severe and beard of formal cut,
Full of wise saws and modern instances;
And so he plays his part. The sixth age shifts
Into the lean and slippered pantaloon
With spectacles on nose and pouch on side,
His youthful hose, well saved, a world too wide
For his shrunk shank, and his big manly voice,
Turning again toward childish treble, pipes
And whistles in his sound. Last scene of all,
That ends this strange eventful history,
Is second childishness and mere oblivion,
Sans teeth, sans eyes, sans taste, sans everything.

The Merchant Of Venice

Act 4 Scene 1

PORTIA

The quality of mercy is not strained.
It droppeth as the gentle rain from heaven
Upon the place beneath. It is twice blest:
It blesseth him that gives and him that takes.
'Tis mightiest in the mightiest; it becomes
The thronèd monarch better than his crown.
His scepter shows the force of temporal power,
The attribute to awe and majesty
Wherein doth sit the dread and fear of kings;
But mercy is above this sceptered sway.
It is enthronèd in the hearts of kings;
It is an attribute to God Himself;
And earthly power doth then show likest God's
When mercy seasons justice. Therefore, Jew,
Though justice be thy plea, consider this:
That in the course of justice none of us
Should see salvation. We do pray for mercy,
And that same prayer doth teach us all to render
The deeds of mercy. I have spoke thus much
To mitigate the justice of thy plea,
Which, if thou follow, this strict court of Venice
Must needs give sentence 'gainst the merchant there.

Hamlet

Act 1 Scene 2

HAMLET

O that this too too solid flesh would melt,
Thaw, and resolve itself into a dew!
Or that the Everlasting had not fix'd
His canon 'gainst self-slaughter! O God! God!
How weary, stale, flat, and unprofitable
Seem to me all the uses of this world!
Fie on't! ah, fie! 'Tis an unweeded garden
That grows to seed; things rank and gross in nature
Possess it merely. That it should come to this!
But two months dead! Nay, not so much, not two.
So excellent a king, that was to this
Hyperion to a satyr; so loving to my mother
That he might not beteem the winds of heaven
Visit her face too roughly. Heaven and earth!
Must I remember? Why, she would hang on him
As if increase of appetite had grown
By what it fed on; and yet, within a month-
Let me not think on't! Frailty, thy name is woman!-
A little month, or ere those shoes were old
With which she followed my poor father's body
Like Niobe, all tears- why she, even she
(O God! a beast that wants discourse of reason
Would have mourn'd longer) married with my uncle;
My father's brother, but no more like my father
Than I to Hercules. Within a month,
Ere yet the salt of most unrighteous tears
Had left the flushing in her galled eyes,
She married. O, most wicked speed, to post
With such dexterity to incestuous sheets!
It is not, nor it cannot come to good.
But break my heart, for I must hold my tongue!

The Tempest

Act 2 Scene 2

TRINCULO

Here's neither bush nor shrub, to bear off any weather at all,
and another storm brewing; I hear it sing i' the wind:
yond same black cloud, yond huge one,
looks like a foul bombard that would shed his liquor.
If it should thunder as it did before,
I know not where to hide my head:
yond same cloud cannot choose but fall by pailfuls.
What have we here? a man or a fish? dead or alive?
A fish: he smells like a fish;
a very ancient and fish-like smell;
a kind of not of the newest Poor-John.
A strange fish! Were I in England now,
as once I was, there would this monster make a man;
any strange beast there makes a man:
when they will not give a doit to relieve a lame beggar,
they will lazy out ten to see a dead Indian.
Legged like a man and his fins like arms!
Warm o' my troth! I do now let loose my opinion;
hold it no longer: this is no fish, but an islander,
that hath lately suffered by a thunderbolt. [Thunder]
Alas, the storm is come again!
my best way is to creep under his gaberdine;
there is no other shelter hereabouts:
misery acquaints a man with strange bed-fellows.
I will here shroud till the dregs of the storm be past.

Hamlet

Act 3 Scene 3

CLAUDIUS

O, my offence is rank, it smells to heaven;
It hath the primal eldest curse upon't,
A brother's murther! Pray can I not,
Though inclination be as sharp as will.
My stronger guilt defeats my strong intent,
And, like a man to double business bound,
I stand in pause where I shall first begin,
And both neglect. What if this cursed hand
Were thicker than itself with brother's blood,
Is there not rain enough in the sweet heavens
To wash it white as snow? Whereto serves mercy
But to confront the visage of offence?
And what's in prayer but this twofold force,
To be forestalled ere we come to fall,
Or pardon'd being down? Then I'll look up;
My fault is past. But, O, what form of prayer
Can serve my turn? 'Forgive me my foul murther'?
That cannot be; since I am still possess'd
Of those effects for which I did the murther-
My crown, mine own ambition, and my queen.
May one be pardon'd and retain th' offence?
In the corrupted currents of this world
Offence's gilded hand may shove by justice,
And oft 'tis seen the wicked prize itself
Buys out the law; but 'tis not so above.
There is no shuffling; there the action lies
In his true nature, and we ourselves compell'd,
Even to the teeth and forehead of our faults,
To give in evidence. What then? What rests?
Try what repentance can. What can it not?

Yet what can it when one cannot repent?
O wretched state! O bosom black as death!
O limed soul, that, struggling to be free,
Art more engag'd! Help, angels! Make assay.
Bow, stubborn knees; and heart with strings of steel,
Be soft as sinews of the new-born babe!
All may be well.

Miles Everett as Claudius in "Hamlet"
photo by Stephen Cihanek • www.Cihanek.com

The Merry Wives of Windsor

Act 3 Scene 5

FALSTAFF

Have I lived to be carried in a basket,
like a barrow of butcher's offal,
and to be thrown in the Thames?
Well, if I be served such another trick,
I'll have my brains ta'en out and buttered,
and give them to a dog for a new-year's gift.
The rogues slighted me into the river
with as little remorse as they would
have drowned a blind bitch's puppies,
fifteen i' the litter:
and you may know by my size
that I have a kind of alacrity in sinking;
if the bottom were as deep as hell,
I should down. I had been drowned,
but that the shore was shelvy and shallow,—
a death that I abhor; for the water swells a man;
and what a thing should I have been
when I had been swelled!
I should have been a mountain of mummy.

Titus Andronicus

Act 5 Scene 1

AARON

Ay, that I had not done a thousand more.
Even now I curse the day—and yet, I think,
Few come within the compass of my curse—
Wherein I did not some notorious ill,
As kill a man, or else devise his death;
Ravish a maid or plot the way to do it;
Accuse some innocent and forswear myself;
Set deadly enmity between two friends;
Make poor men's cattle break their necks;
Set fire on barns and haystalks in the night,
And bid the owners quench them with their tears.
Oft have I digged up dead men from their graves
And set them upright at their dear friends' door,
Even when their sorrows almost was forgot,
And on their skins, as on the bark of trees,
Have with my knife carvèd in Roman letters
"Let not your sorrow die, though I am dead."
But I have done a thousand dreadful things
As willingly as one would kill a fly,
And nothing grieves me heartily indeed
But that I cannot do ten thousand more.

Jennifer Wallace as Ophelia in "Hamlet"
photo by Stephen Cihanek • www.Cihanek.com

Hamlet

Act 2 Scene 1

OPHELIA

Oh my Lord, my Lord...
As I was sewing in my closet,
Lord Hamlet, with his doublet all unbrac'd,
No hat upon his head, his stockings foul'd,
Ungart'red, and down-gyved to his ankle;
Pale as his shirt, his knees knocking each other,
And with a look so piteous in purport
As if he had been loosed out of hell
To speak of horrors - he comes before me.
He took me by the wrist and held me hard;
Then goes he to the length of all his arm,
And, with his other hand thus o'er his brow,
He falls to such perusal of my face
As he would draw it. Long stay'd he so.
At last, a little shaking of mine arm,
And thrice his head thus waving up and down,
He rais'd a sigh so piteous and profound
As it did seem to shatter all his bulk
And end his being. That done, he lets me go,
And with his head over his shoulder turn'd
He seem'd to find his way without his eyes,
For out o' doors he went without their help
And to the last bended their light on me.

Macbeth

Act 1 Scene 7

MACBETH

If it were done when 'tis done, then 'twere well
It were done quickly: if the assassination
Could trammel up the consequence, and catch
With his surcease success; that but this blow
Might be the be-all and the end-all here,
But here, upon this bank and shoal of time,
We'ld jump the life to come. But in these cases
We still have judgment here; that we but teach
Bloody instructions, which, being taught, return
To plague the inventor: this even-handed justice
Commends the ingredients of our poison'd chalice
To our own lips. He's here in double trust;
First, as I am his kinsman and his subject,
Strong both against the deed; then, as his host,
Who should against his murderer shut the door,
Not bear the knife myself. Besides, this Duncan
Hath borne his faculties so meek, hath been
So clear in his great office, that his virtues
Will plead like angels, trumpet-tongued, against
The deep damnation of his taking-off;
And pity, like a naked new-born babe,
Striding the blast, or heaven's cherubim, horsed
Upon the sightless couriers of the air,
Shall blow the horrid deed in every eye,
That tears shall drown the wind. I have no spur
To prick the sides of my intent, but only
Vaulting ambition, which o'erleaps itself
And falls on the other.

Romeo & Juliet

Act 1 Scene 3

NURSE

Even or odd, of all days in the year,
Come Lammas-eve at night shall she be fourteen.
Susan and she.God rest all Christian souls!.
Were of an age: well, Susan is with God;
She was too good for me: but, as I said,
On Lammas-eve at night shall she be fourteen;
That shall she, marry; I remember it well.
'Tis since the earthquake now eleven years;
And she was wean'd,.I never shall forget it,.
Of all the days of the year, upon that day:
For I had then laid wormwood to my dug,
Sitting in the sun under the dove-house wall;
My lord and you were then at Mantua:.
Nay, I do bear a brain:.but, as I said,
When it did taste the wormwood on the nipple
Of my dug and felt it bitter, pretty fool,
To see it tetchy and fall out with the dug!
And since that time it is eleven years;
For then she could stand alone; nay, by the rood,
She could have run and waddled all about;
For even the day before, she broke her brow:
And then my husband - God be with his soul!
A' was a merry man - took up the child:
'Yea,' quoth he, 'dost thou fall upon thy face?
Thou wilt fall backward when thou hast more wit;
Wilt thou not, Jule?' and, by my holidame,
The pretty wretch left crying and said 'Ay.'
To see, now, how a jest shall come about!
I warrant, an I should live a thousand years,
I never should forget it

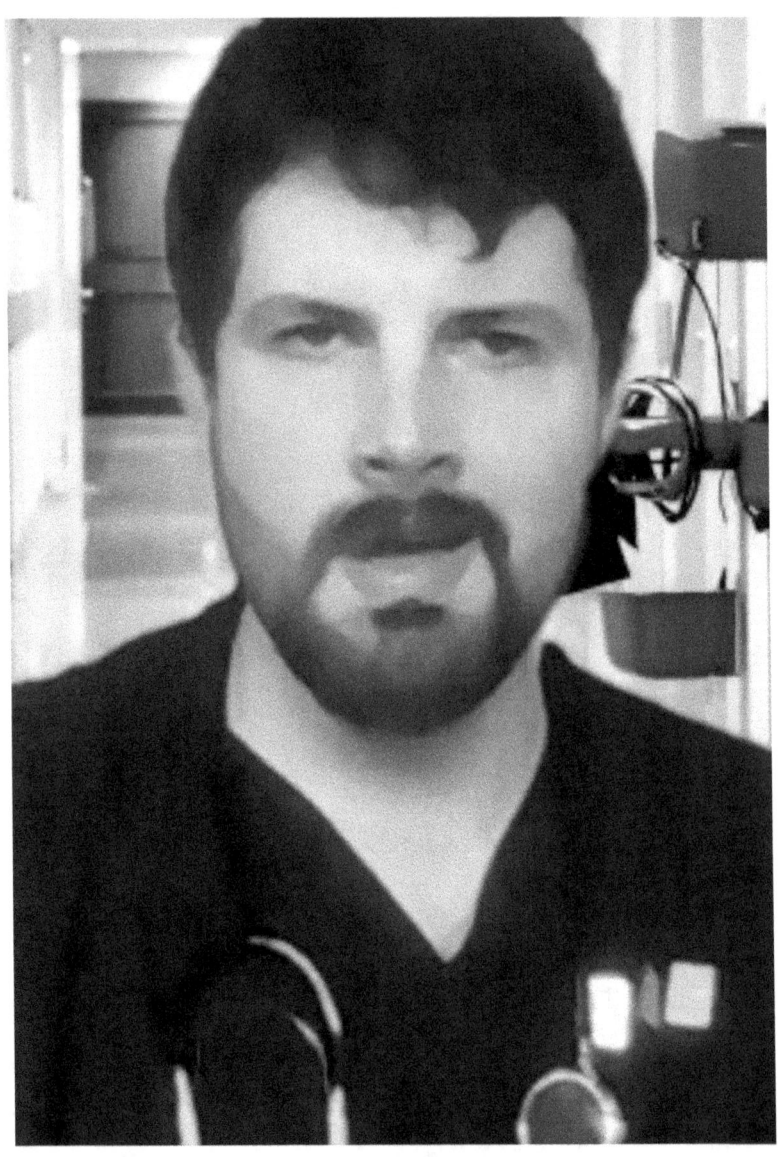

*Thomas Samuels as Chorus in a pandemic era virtual "Henry V,"
photo courtesy of Thomas Samuels*

Henry V

Prologue

CHORUS

O for a Muse of fire, that would ascend
The brightest heaven of invention,
A kingdom for a stage, princes to act
And monarchs to behold the swelling scene!
Then should the warlike Harry, like himself,
Assume the port of Mars; and at his heels,
Leash'd in like hounds, should famine, sword and fire
Crouch for employment. But pardon, and gentles all,
The flat unraised spirits that have dared
On this unworthy scaffold to bring forth
So great an object: can this cockpit hold
The vasty fields of France? or may we cram
Within this wooden O the very casques
That did affright the air at Agincourt?
O, pardon! since a crooked figure may
Attest in little place a million;
And let us, ciphers to this great accompt,
On your imaginary forces work.
Suppose within the girdle of these walls
Are now confined two mighty monarchies,
Whose high upreared and abutting fronts
The perilous narrow ocean parts asunder:
Piece out our imperfections with your thoughts;
Into a thousand parts divide on man,
And make imaginary puissance;
Think when we talk of horses, that you see them
Printing their proud hoofs i' the receiving earth;
For 'tis your thoughts that now must deck our kings,
Carry them here and there; jumping o'er times,

Turning the accomplishment of many years
Into an hour-glass: for the which supply,
Admit me Chorus to this history;
Who prologue-like your humble patience pray,
Gently to hear, kindly to judge, our play.

Measure For Measure

Act 2 Scene 4

ISABELLA

To whom should I complain? Did I tell this,
Who would believe me? O perilous mouths,
That bear in them one and the self-same tongue,
Either of condemnation or approof;
Bidding the law make court'sy to their will:
Hooking both right and wrong to the appetite,
To follow as it draws! I'll to my brother:
Though he hath fallen by prompture of the blood,
Yet hath he in him such a mind of honour.
That, had he twenty heads to tender down
On twenty bloody blocks, he'ld yield them up,
Before his sister should her body stoop
To such abhorr'd pollution.
Then, Isabel, live chaste, and, brother, die:
More than our brother is our chastity.
I'll tell him yet of Angelo's request,
And fit his mind to death, for his soul's rest.

*Sean Gorman as Orsino with Jennifer Wallace as Viola, in "Twelfth Night"
photo by Stephen Cihanek • www.Cihanek.com*

Twelfth Night

Act 1 Scene 1

ORSINO

If music be the food of love, play on;
Give me excess of it, that, surfeiting,
The appetite may sicken, and so die.
That strain again! it had a dying fall:
O, it came o'er my ear like the sweet sound,
That breathes upon a bank of violets,
Stealing and giving odour! Enough; no more:
'Tis not so sweet now as it was before.
O spirit of love! how quick and fresh art thou,
That, notwithstanding thy capacity
Receiveth as the sea, nought enters there,
Of what validity and pitch soe'er,
But falls into abatement and low price,
Even in a minute: so full of shapes is fancy
That it alone is high fantastical.

As You Like It

Act 3 Scene 5

PHEBE

Think not I love him, though I ask for him.
'Tis but a peevish boy; yet he talks well;
But what care I for words? yet words do well,
When he that speaks them pleases those that hear.
It is a pretty youth: not very pretty:
But, sure, he's proud; and yet his pride becomes him:
He'll make a proper man: the best thing in him
Is his complexion; and faster than his tongue
Did make offence his eye did heal it up.
He is not very tall; yet for his years he's tall:
His leg is but so so; and yet 'tis well:
There was a pretty redness in his lip,
A little riper and more lusty red
Than that mix'd in his cheek; 'twas just the difference
Betwixt the constant red and mingled damask.
There be some women, Silvius, had they mark'd him
In parcels as I did, would have gone near
To fall in love with him; but, for my part,
I love him not nor hate him not; and yet
Have more cause to hate him than to love him:
For what had he to do to chide at me?
He said mine eyes were black and my hair black;
And, now I am remember'd, scorn'd at me.
I marvel why I answer'd not again:
But that's all one; omittance is no quittance.
I'll write to him a very taunting letter,
And thou shalt bear it: wilt thou, Silvius?

The Merchant of Venice

Act 3 Scene 1

SHYLOCK

There I have another bad match! A bankrout,
a prodigal, who dare scarce show his head on
the Rialto, a beggar that was used to come so smug
upon the mart! Let him look to his bond.
He was wont to call me usurer; let him look to his bond.
He was wont to lend money for a Christian cur'sy;
let him look to his bond. He hath disgraced me,
and hindered me half a million; laughed at my losses,
mocked at my gains, scorned my nation,
thwarted my bargains, cooled my friends,
heated mine enemies; and what's his reason?
I am a Jew. Hath not a Jew eyes?
hath not a Jew hands, organs, dimensions,
senses, affections, passions? fed with the same food,
hurt with the same weapons, subject to the same diseases,
healed by the same means, warmed and cooled
by the same winter and summer, as a Christian is?
If you prick us, do we not bleed?
if you tickle us, do we not laugh?
if you poison us, do we not die?
and if you wrong us, shall we not revenge?
If we are like you in the rest,
we will resemble you in that.
If a Jew wrong a Christian, what is his humility?
Revenge. If a Christian wrong a Jew,
what should his sufferance be by Christian example?
Why, revenge. The villany you teach me,
I will execute, and it shall go hard
but I will better the instruction.

Richard III

Act 1 Scene 2

RICHARD

Was ever woman in this humor wooed?
Was ever woman in this humor won?
I'll have her, but I will not keep her long.
What, I that killed her husband and his father,
To take her in her heart's extremest hate,
With curses in her mouth, tears in her eyes,
The bleeding witness of my hatred by,
Having God, her conscience, and these bars against me,
And I no friends to back my suit at all
But the plain devil and dissembling looks?
And yet to win her, all the world to nothing!
Ha!
Hath she forgot already that brave prince,
Edward, her lord, whom I some three months since
Stabbed in my angry mood at Tewkesbury?
A sweeter and a lovelier gentleman,
Framed in the prodigality of nature,
Young, valiant, wise, and, no doubt, right royal,
The spacious world cannot again afford.
And will she yet abase her eyes on me,
That cropped the golden prime of this sweet prince
And made her widow to a woeful bed?
On me, whose all not equals Edward's moiety?
On me, that halts and am misshapen thus?
My dukedom to a beggarly denier,
I do mistake my person all this while!
Upon my life, she finds, although I cannot,
Myself to be a marv'lous proper man.
I'll be at charges for a looking glass
And entertain a score or two of tailors

To study fashions to adorn my body.
Since I am crept in favor with myself,
I will maintain it with some little cost.
But first I'll turn yon fellow in his grave
And then return lamenting to my love.
Shine out, fair sun, till I have bought a glass,
That I may see my shadow as I pass.

Hamlet

Act 4 Scene 7

GERTRUDE

There is a willow grows aslant a brook,
That shows his hoary leaves in the glassy stream.
There with fantastic garlands did she make—
Of crowflowers, nettles, daisies, and long purples,
That liberal shepherds give a grosser name,
But our cold maids do dead men's fingers call them.
There on the pendant boughs her coronet weeds
Clamb'ring to hang, an envious sliver broke,
When down her weedy trophies and herself
Fell in the weeping brook. Her clothes spread wide
And, mermaid-like, awhile they bore her up;
Which time she chaunted snatches of old tunes,
As one incapable of her own distress,
Or like a creature native and indued
Unto that element; but long it could not be
Till that her garments, heavy with their drink,
Pull'd the poor wretch from her melodious lay
To muddy death.

Henry V

Act 3 Scene 1

HENRY

Once more unto the breach, dear friends, once more;
Or close the wall up with our English dead.
In peace there's nothing so becomes a man
As modest stillness and humility:
But when the blast of war blows in our ears,
Then imitate the action of the tiger;
Stiffen the sinews, summon up the blood,
Disguise fair nature with hard-favour'd rage;
Then lend the eye a terrible aspect;
Let pry through the portage of the head
Like the brass cannon; let the brow o'erwhelm it
As fearfully as doth a galled rock
O'erhang and jutty his confounded base,
Swill'd with the wild and wasteful ocean.
Now set the teeth and stretch the nostril wide,
Hold hard the breath and bend up every spirit
To his full height. On, on, you noblest English.
Whose blood is fet from fathers of war-proof!
Fathers that, like so many Alexanders,
Have in these parts from morn till even fought
And sheathed their swords for lack of argument:
Dishonour not your mothers; now attest
That those whom you call'd fathers did beget you.
Be copy now to men of grosser blood,
And teach them how to war. And you, good yeoman,
Whose limbs were made in England, show us here
The mettle of your pasture; let us swear
That you are worth your breeding; which I doubt not;
For there is none of you so mean and base,
That hath not noble lustre in your eyes.
I see you stand like greyhounds in the slips,
Straining upon the start. The game's afoot:
Follow your spirit, and upon this charge
Cry 'God for Harry, England, and Saint George!'

Two Nobel Kinsmen

Act 2 Scene 4

JAILOR'S DAUGHTER

Why should I love this gentleman? 'Tis odds
He never will affect me. I am base,
My father the mean keeper of his prison,
And he a prince. To marry him is hopeless;
To be his whore is witless. Out upon 't!
What pushes are we wenches driven to
When fifteen once has found us! First, I saw him;
I, seeing, thought he was a goodly man;
He has as much to please a woman in him,
If he please to bestow it so, as ever
These eyes yet looked on. Next, I pitied him,
And so would any young wench, o' my conscience,
That ever dreamed, or vowed her maidenhead
To a young handsome man. Then I loved him,
Extremely loved him, infinitely loved him!

And yet he had a cousin, fair as he too.
But in my heart was Palamon, and there,
Lord, what a coil he keeps! To hear him
Sing in an evening, what a heaven it is!
And yet his songs are sad ones. Fairer spoken
Was never gentleman. When I come in
To bring him water in a morning, first
He bows his noble body, then salutes me thus:
"Fair, gentle maid, good morrow. May thy goodness
Get thee a happy husband." Once he kissed me;
I loved my lips the better ten days after.

Would he would do so ev'ry day! He grieves much—
And me as much to see his misery.
What should I do to make him know I love him?
For I would fain enjoy him. Say I ventured
To set him free? What says the law then?
Thus much for law or kindred! I will do it,
And this night, or tomorrow, he shall love me.

Antony & Cleopatra

Act 2 Scene 2

ENOBARBUS

The barge she sat in, like a burnish'd throne,
Burn'd on the water: the poop was beaten gold;
Purple the sails, and so perfumed that
The winds were love-sick with them; the oars were silver,
Which to the tune of flutes kept stroke, and made
The water which they beat to follow faster,
As amorous of their strokes. For her own person,
It beggar'd all description: she did lie
In her pavilion.cloth-of-gold of tissue.
O'er-picturing that Venus where we see
The fancy outwork nature: on each side her
Stood pretty dimpled boys, like smiling Cupids,
With divers-colour'd fans, whose wind did seem
To glow the delicate cheeks which they did cool,
And what they undid did.

Her gentlewomen, like the Nereides,
So many mermaids, tended her i' the eyes,
And made their bends adornings: at the helm
A seeming mermaid steers: the silken tackle
Swell with the touches of those flower-soft hands,
That yarely frame the office. From the barge
A strange invisible perfume hits the sense
Of the adjacent wharfs. The city cast
Her people out upon her; and Antony,
Enthroned i' the market-place, did sit alone,
Whistling to the air; which, but for vacancy,
Had gone to gaze on Cleopatra too,
And made a gap in nature.
Upon her landing, Antony sent to her,

Invited her to supper: she replied,
It should be better he became her guest;
Which she entreated: our courteous Antony,
Whom ne'er the word of 'No' woman heard speak,
Being barber'd ten times o'er, goes to the feast,
And for his ordinary pays his heart
For what his eyes eat only.

I saw her once
Hop forty paces through the public street;
And having lost her breath, she spoke, and panted,
That she did make defect perfection,
And, breathless, power breathe forth.

Age cannot wither her, nor custom stale
Her infinite variety: other women cloy
The appetites they feed: but she makes hungry
Where most she satisfies; for vilest things
Become themselves in her: that the holy priests
Bless her when she is riggish.

Twelfth Night

Act 2 Scene 2

VIOLA

I left no ring with her: what means this lady?
Fortune forbid my outside have not charm'd her!
She made good view of me; indeed, so much,
That sure methought her eyes had lost her tongue,
For she did speak in starts distractedly.
She loves me, sure; the cunning of her passion
Invites me in this churlish messenger.
None of my lord's ring! why, he sent her none.
I am the man: if it be so, as 'tis,
Poor lady, she were better love a dream.
Disguise, I see, thou art a wickedness,
Wherein the pregnant enemy does much.
How easy is it for the proper-false
In women's waxen hearts to set their forms!
Alas, our frailty is the cause, not we!
For such as we are made of, such we be.
How will this fadge? my master loves her dearly;
And I, poor monster, fond as much on him;
And she, mistaken, seems to dote on me.
What will become of this? As I am man,
My state is desperate for my master's love;
As I am woman,.now alas the day!.
What thriftless sighs shall poor Olivia breathe!
O time! thou must untangle this, not I;
It is too hard a knot for me to untie!

Henry VI Pt. 1

Act 1 Scene 2

JOAN LA PUCELLE

Dauphin, I am by birth a shepherd's daughter,
My wit untrain'd in any kind of art.
Heaven and our Lady gracious hath it pleased
To shine on my contemptible estate:
Lo, whilst I waited on my tender lambs,
And to sun's parching heat display'd my cheeks,
God's mother deigned to appear to me
And in a vision full of majesty
Will'd me to leave my base vocation
And free my country from calamity:
Her aid she promised and assured success:
In complete glory she reveal'd herself;
And, whereas I was black and swart before,
With those clear rays which she infused on me
That beauty am I bless'd with which you see.
Ask me what question thou canst possible,
And I will answer unpremeditated:
My courage try by combat, if thou darest,
And thou shalt find that I exceed my sex.
Resolve on this, thou shalt be fortunate,
If thou receive me for thy warlike mate.

Sean Latasa as Malvolio in "Twelfth Night"
photo by Stephen Cihanek • www.Cihanek.com

Twelfth Night

Act 2 Scene 5

MALVOLIO

By my life, this is my lady's hand!
These be her very c's, her u's, and her t's,
and thus she makes her great P's.
It is in contempt of question her hand.

To the unknown beloved, this, and my
good wishes—Her very phrases! By your leave, wax.
Soft. And the impressure her Lucrece, with which
she uses to seal—'tis my lady! *[He opens the letter]*
To whom should this be?

>Jove knows I love,
>   But who?
>Lips, do not move;
>   No man must know.

"No man must know." What follows? The numbers altered.
"No man must know." If this should be thee, Malvolio!

>I may command where I adore,
>   But silence, like a Lucrece knife,
>With bloodless stroke my heart doth gore;
>   M.O.A.I. doth sway my life.

"M.O.A.I. doth sway my life." Nay, but first
let me see, let me see, let me see.

"I may command where I adore." Why, she
may command me; I serve her; she is my lady. Why,
this is evident to any formal capacity. There is no
obstruction in this. And the end--what should that

alphabetical position portend? If I could make that
resemble something in me! Softly! "M.O.A.I."—

"M"--Malvolio. "M"—why, that begins my name!
"M." But then there is no consonancy in
the sequel that suffers under probation. "A" should
follow, but "O" does.
And then "I" comes behind.

"M.O.A.I." This simulation is not as the former,
and yet to crush this a little, it would bow to me,
for every one of these letters are in my name.
Soft, here follows prose.

[He reads] If this fall into thy hand, revolve.
In my stars I am above thee, but be not afraid of greatness.
Some are born great, some achieve greatness, and
some have greatness thrust upon 'em. Thy fates open
their hands. Let thy blood and spirit embrace them.
And, to inure thyself to what thou art like to be,
 cast off thy humble slough and appear fresh. Be opposite
with a kinsman, surly with servants. Let thy tongue tang
arguments of state. Put thyself into the trick of singularity.
She thus advises thee that sighs for thee.

Remember who commended thy yellow stockings and
wished to see thee ever cross-gartered. I say, remember.
Go to, thou art made, if thou desir'st to be so.
If not, let me see thee a steward still, the fellow of servants,
and not worthy to touch Fortune's fingers.
Farewell. She that would alter services with thee,
The Fortunate-Unhappy.

Daylight and champagne discovers not more! This is open.
I will be proud, I will read politic authors,
I will baffle Sir Toby, I will wash off gross acquaintance,

I will be point-devise the very man.
I do not now fool myself, to let imagination jade me;
for every reason excites to this, that my lady loves me.
She did commend my yellow stockings of late,
she did praise my leg being cross-gartered,
and in this she manifests herself to my love and,
with a kind of injunction, drives me to these habits of her liking.
I thank my stars, I am happy. I will be strange, stout,
in yellow stockings, and cross-gartered, even with
the swiftness of putting on. Jove and my stars be praised!
Here is yet a postscript.

[He reads] Thou canst not choose but know who I am.
If thou entertain'st my love, let it appear in thy smiling;
thy smiles become thee well. Therefore in my presence
still smile, dear my sweet, I prithee.

Jove, I thank thee! I will smile.
I will do everything that thou wilt have me.

Henry VI Pt. 3

Act 1 Scene 4

QUEEN MARGARET

Brave warriors, Clifford and Northumberland,
Come, make him stand upon this molehill here
That raught at mountains with outstretchèd arms,
Yet parted but the shadow with his hand.
[They place York on a small prominence.]
What, was it you that would be England's king?
Was 't you that reveled in our parliament
And made a preachment of your high descent?
Where are your mess of sons to back you now,
The wanton Edward and the lusty George?
And where's that valiant crookback prodigy,
Dickie, your boy, that with his grumbling voice
Was wont to cheer his dad in mutinies?
Or, with the rest, where is your darling Rutland?
Look, York, I stained this napkin with the blood
That valiant Clifford with his rapier's point
Made issue from the bosom of the boy;
And if thine eyes can water for his death,
I give thee this to dry thy cheeks withal.
[She gives him a bloody cloth.]
Alas, poor York, but that I hate thee deadly
I should lament thy miserable state.
I prithee grieve to make me merry, York.
What, hath thy fiery heart so parched thine entrails
That not a tear can fall for Rutland's death?
Why art thou patient, man? Thou shouldst be mad;
And I, to make thee mad, do mock thee thus.
Stamp, rave, and fret, that I may sing and dance.
Thou would'st be fee'd, I see, to make me sport.—
York cannot speak unless he wear a crown.

A crown for York! *[She is handed a paper crown.]*
And, lords, bow low to him.
Hold you his hands whilst I do set it on.
[She puts the crown on York's head.]
Ay, marry, sir, now looks he like a king.
Ay, this is he that took King Henry's chair,
And this is he was his adopted heir.
But how is it that great Plantagenet
Is crowned so soon and broke his solemn oath?—
As I bethink me, you should not be king
Till our King Henry had shook hands with Death.
And will you pale your head in Henry's glory
And rob his temples of the diadem
Now, in his life, against your holy oath?
O, 'tis a fault too too unpardonable.
Off with the crown and, with the crown, his head;
And whilst we breathe, take time to do him dead.

*Lyra Wilder as a fairy in "A Midsummer Night's Dream"
photo by Agnes Fohn*

A Midsummer Night's Dream

Act 2 Scene 1

FIRST FAIRY

Over hill, over dale,
Thorough bush, thorough brier,
Over park, over pale,
Thorough flood, thorough fire;
I do wander everywhere,
Swifter than the moon's sphere.
And I serve the Fairy Queen,
To dew her orbs upon the green.
The cowslips tall her pensioners be;
In their gold coats spots you see;
Those be rubies, fairy favors;
In those freckles live their savors.
I must go seek some dewdrops here
And hang a pearl in every cowslip's ear.
Farewell, thou lob of spirits. I'll be gone.
Our queen and all her elves come here anon.

Thomas Samuels as Hamlet
photo by Stephen Cihanek • www.Cihanek.com

Hamlet

Act 2 Scene 2

HAMLET

O what a rogue and peasant slave am I!
Is it not monstrous that this player here,
But in a fiction, in a dream of passion,
Could force his soul so to his own conceit
That, from her working, all his visage wann'd,
Tears in his eyes, distraction in's aspect,
A broken voice, and his whole function suiting
With forms to his conceit? And all for nothing!
For Hecuba!
What's Hecuba to him, or he to Hecuba,
That he should weep for her? What would he do,
Had he the motive and the cue for passion
That I have? He would drown the stage with tears
And cleave the general ear with horrid speech;
Make mad the guilty and appal the free,
Confound the ignorant, and amaze indeed
The very faculties of eyes and ears.
Yet I,
A dull and muddy-mettled rascal, peak
Like John-a-dreams, unpregnant of my cause,
And can say nothing! No, not for a king,
Upon whose property and most dear life
A damn'd defeat was made. Am I a coward?
Who calls me villain? breaks my pate across?
Plucks off my beard and blows it in my face?
Tweaks me by th' nose? gives me the lie i' th' throat
As deep as to the lungs? Who does me this, ha?
'Swounds, I should take it! for it cannot be
But I am pigeon-liver'd and lack gall
To make oppression bitter, or ere this

I should have fatted all the region kites
With this slave's offal. Bloody bawdy villain!
Remorseless, treacherous, lecherous, kindless villain!
O, vengeance!
Why, what an ass am I! This is most brave,
That I, the son of a dear father murder'd,
Prompted to my revenge by heaven and hell,
Must (like a whore) unpack my heart with words
And fall a-cursing like a very drab,
A scullion!
Fie upon't! foh! About, my brain! Hum, I have heard
That guilty creatures, sitting at a play,
Have by the very cunning of the scene
Been struck so to the soul that presently
They have proclaim'd their malefactions;
For murder, though it have no tongue, will speak
With most miraculous organ, I'll have these Players
Play something like the murder of my father
Before mine uncle. I'll observe his looks;
I'll tent him to the quick. If he but blench,
I know my course. The spirit that I have seen
May be a devil; and the devil hath power
T' assume a pleasing shape; yea, and perhaps
Out of my weakness and my melancholy,
As he is very potent with such spirits,
Abuses me to damn me. I'll have grounds
More relative than this. The play's the thing
Wherein I'll catch the conscience of the King.

Richard II

Act 3 Scene 2

RICHARD

Of comfort no man speak.
Let's talk of graves, of worms, and epitaphs,
Make dust our paper, and with rainy eyes
Write sorrow on the bosom of the earth.
Let's choose executors and talk of wills.
And yet not so, for what can we bequeath
Save our deposèd bodies to the ground?

Our lands, our lives, and all are Bolingbroke's,
And nothing can we call our own but death
And that small model of the barren earth
Which serves as paste and cover to our bones.

For God's sake, let us sit upon the ground
And tell sad stories of the death of kings—
How some have been deposed, some slain in war,
Some haunted by the ghosts they have deposed,
Some poisoned by their wives, some sleeping killed,
All murdered. For within the hollow crown
That rounds the mortal temples of a king
Keeps Death his court, and there the antic sits,
Scoffing his state and grinning at his pomp,
Allowing him a breath, a little scene,
To monarchize, be feared, and kill with looks,
Infusing him with self and vain conceit,
As if this flesh which walls about our life
Were brass impregnable; and humored thus,
Comes at the last and with a little pin
Bores through his castle wall, and farewell, king!

Cover your heads, and mock not flesh and blood
With solemn reverence. Throw away respect,
Tradition, form, and ceremonious duty,
For you have but mistook me all this while.
I live with bread like you, feel want,
Taste grief, need friends. Subjected thus,
How can you say to me I am a king?

Nana Visitor as Richard II
photo courtesy of Nana Visitor

As You Like It

Epilogue

ROSALIND

It is not the fashion to see the lady the epilogue, but it is no more unhandsome than to see the lord the prologue. If it be true that good wine needs no bush, 'tis true that a good play needs no epilogue. Yet to good wine they do use good bushes, and good plays prove the better by the help of good epilogues. What a case am I in then that am neither a good epilogue nor cannot insinuate with you in the behalf of a good play! I am not furnished like a beggar; therefore to beg will not become me. My way is to conjure you, and I'll begin with the women. I charge you, O women, for the love you bear to men, to like as much of this play as please you. And I charge you, O men, for the love you bear to women—as I perceive by your simpering, none of you hates them—that between you and the women the play may please. If I were a woman, I would kiss as many of you as had beards that pleased me, complexions that liked me, and breaths that I defied not. And I am sure as many as have good beards, or good faces, or sweet breaths will for my kind offer, when I make curtsy, bid me farewell.

Get all 3!

Shakespeare for Contemporary Theatre

Volume 1

Macbeth

A Midsummer Night's Dream

Henry V

Shakespeare for Contemporary Theatre

Volume 2

Richard II

The Taming of the Shrew

Hamlet

Available at your favorite bookstore or online at www.local-author.com

www.ingramcontent.com/pod-product-compliance
Lightning Source LLC
LaVergne TN
LVHW021239080526
838199LV00088B/4753